Creative Storage Solutions
for Your Home

Rick Williams

POPULAR WOODWORKING BOOKS
CINCINNATI, OHIO
www.popularwoodworking.com

Read This Important Safety Notice

To prevent accidents, keep safety in mind while you work. Use the safety guards installed on power equipment; they are for your protection. When working on power equipment, keep fingers away from saw blades, wear safety goggles to prevent injuries from flying wood chips and sawdust, wear headphones to protect your hearing and consider installing a dust vacuum to reduce the amount of airborne sawdust in your woodshop. Don't wear loose clothing, such as neckties or shirts with loose sleeves, or jewelry, such as rings, necklaces or bracelets, when working on power equipment. Tie back long hair to prevent it from getting caught in your equipment. People who are sensitive to certain chemicals should check the chemical content of any product before using it. The authors and editors who compiled this book have tried to make the contents as accurate and correct as possible. Plans, illustrations, photographs and text have been carefully checked. All instructions, plans and projects should be carefully read, studied and understood before beginning construction. Due to the variability of local conditions, construction materials, skill levels, etc., neither the author nor Popular Woodworking Books assumes any responsibility for any accidents, injuries, damages or other losses incurred resulting from the material presented in this book. Prices listed for supplies and equipment were current at the time of publication and are subject to change. All glass shelving should have all edges polished and must be tempered. Untempered glass shelves will shatter and can cause serious bodily injury. Tempered shelves are very strong and if they do break, they will just crumble, minimizing personal injury.

Metric Conversion Chart

TO CONVERT	TO	MULTIPLY BY
Inches	Centimeters	2.54
Centimeters	Inches	0.4
Feet	Centimeters	30.5
Centimeters	Feet	0.03
Yards	Meters	0.9
Meters	Yards	1.1
Sq. Inches	Sq. Centimeters	6.45
Sq. Centimeters	Sq. Inches	0.16
Sq. Feet	Sq. Meters	0.09
Sq. Meters	Sq. Feet	10.8
Sq. Yards	Sq. Meters	0.8
Sq. Meters	Sq. Yards	1.2
Pounds	Kilograms	0.45
Kilograms	Pounds	2.2
Ounces	Grams	28.4
Grams	Ounces	0.035

Creative Storage Solutions for Your Home. Copyright © 2002 by Rick Williams. Manufactured in China. All rights reserved. No part of this book may be reproduced in any form or by any electronic or mechanical means, including information storage and retrieval systems, without permission in writing from the publisher, except by a reviewer, who may quote brief passages in a review. Published by Popular Woodworking Books, an imprint of F&W Publications, Inc., 4700 E. Galbraith Road, Cincinnati, Ohio, 45236. First edition.

Visit our Web site at www.popularwoodworking.com for more information and resources for woodworkers.

Other fine Popular Woodworking Books are available from your local bookstore or direct from the publisher.

06   05   04   03   5   4   3   2

Library of Congress Cataloging-in-Publication Data
Williams, Rick
Creative storage solution for your home / by Rick Williams
p. cm.
Includes index.
ISBN 1-55870-594-5 (alk. paper)
1. Furniture making. 2. Storage in the home. I. Title

TT194.W55 2001
684.1'6--dc21

Edited by Jennifer Churchill and Ryan Williams
Designed by Brian Roeth
Page layout by Kathy Bergstrom
Lead photography by Al Parrish
Step-by-step photography by Rick Williams
Production coordinated by Mark Griffin
Technical illustrations by Len Churchill
Acquisitions editor: Jim Stack

About the Author

Rick Williams is a general building contractor and custom cabinetmaker by trade. He specializes in custom homes and unique additions, of which the owners may say something like, "I remember this or that when I was a kid; can we do something like that here?" After building a variety of such things that were specifically tailored to individuals, he has learned to expand on what may be considered the conventional way of woodworking.

Dedication

This book is dedicated to my wife, Dee, my son, Ryan, and my daughter, Rikki, whose help and encouragement are always there for me.

Acknowledgments

First, I would like to thank my 13-year-old son, Ryan, who is my personal editor and writer. Without his help, I still would be slowly pecking, one finger at a time, on the computer keyboard to write this book.

I would also like to thank my editor, Jim Stack, for giving me the opportunity to write this book and for leading me through the process one step at a time. My thanks also go to photographer Al Parrish, who made my work look better than I ever could. Many thanks also to Jennifer Churchill, whom I've never met, but who has done a great job sorting out all of the things I've written.

My appreciation goes out to all of the rest of the folks at Popular Woodworking Books who worked to put this book together.

In my building career, I've been fortunate enough to have worked for a lot of great people who have challenged me to be creative while I was designing and building for them. For this, I am forever grateful.

Two of these people are Ron and Fran Stolich, whom I've had the pleasure of working for more than anyone else in my career. Fran has the unique ability to picture things that will be perfectly suited to their home, and I am grateful to have had the chance to build a few of her ideas. One of those ideas is the built-in bookcase in chapter 10.

Two others are Frank and Connie Andermahr, whose small addition to their home evolved into the crowning jewel of my career. In the same way Al Parrish improved my projects with his photography skills, James Mailloux, the master of cement plastering, really gave the Andermahrs' home its unique character. The hall tree seat and the display case in this book are current residents of that home.

Many thanks to everyone I've worked for over the years.

project kids: a labor of love

More than five years ago, Rick Williams was a scoutleader for his son's Cub Scout pack. All of their Scout meetings took place in Rick's woodshop, a room that fascinated the group of boys. The pride and satisfaction the group seemed to acquire from building small projects inspired Rick to build his own personal "field of dreams." Investing their own time and money, Rick and his wife, DeEtta, purchased a 25'-long trailer and outfitted it with nine small workbenches. Calling it Project Kids, Rick took his trailer on the road to local elementary schools, senior care centers and other locations. The focus of Project Kids is on disabled or handicapped children, disadvantaged children, continuing education students and senior citizens at care facilities. The goal of Project Kids is to provide kids of all ages and disabilities the opportunity to realize for themselves the joy, pride and sense of accomplishment in building something with their own hands. Rick offers this service for free to any child or adult who can benefit from it, and he organizes sessions around his busy work schedule. The Williamses invest their own money into Project Kids;

some minimal donations have been offered to them, as well. Some day, Rick hopes to be sponsored by a corporation in order to continue his work with Project Kids and to expand the service area and capabilities of Project Kids.

All of the wooden toys that are created by participants at the nine Project Kids workbench stations are partially precut and prepped by Rick and his volunteers. Rick wants the participants to learn something about woodworking, but he also wants to be sure each child is able to finish their project and experience the feeling of self-sufficiency and pride that comes with a completed toy. "They cut out the final pieces themselves, under my supervision, of course, and then they do the drilling and sanding." Each workstation in the trailer is equipped with a hammer, a saw, a screwdriver, a square, a hand drill, a sanding block and safety glasses. Rick has circulated the Project Kids trailer throughout Calaveras County in north-central Cali-

fornia, where he lives; but he has bigger dreams. He's had requests to bring his trailer to Los Angeles, San Francisco and elsewhere in his home state. Each time he offers a session, he receives two or three requests from other organizations. Although it's called Project Kids, Rick often offers his traveling workshop to senior care centers. "I've had kids from age 2 through age 92," he says. His most difficult obstacle in sharing Project Kids is his day job as a contractor; scheduling weekday sessions is often a conflict, but he fits in every appointment he possibly can. "The kids' energy is boundless, and that's my reward," he says. "The experience of Project Kids is just so awesome; I could talk about it for days!" Rick welcomes any queries about Project Kids; he can be contacted at:

Project Kids
P.O. Box 1285
Murphys, California 95247
Fax: 209-728-3769
bodee@sonnet.com.

table of contents

introduction

If you have what I call the six basic woodworking tools, you can build almost any piece of furniture you can buy. You may have to be a little flexible on design, but rest assured it will look great!

Please do not get me wrong — I like tools — and I have my fair share. In fact, my wife says I am like a kid in a candy store when I am in a tool store. But the reality is we do not need every new tool that is created in order to build professional-looking furniture that will last to be passed down through generations. But don't tell my wife that, or she might not let me go to the candy, I mean, tool store anymore!

In the introductory chapter, "Alternative Woodworking Methods," I will describe how to build an alternative raised panel door, which also can be used as an end or side panel on almost any piece of furniture. I will also show you an alternative to a flat tabletop to add a look of quality and craftsmanship to your woodworking projects.

You probably already have the tools needed to build these projects: **a table saw, a belt sander, a jigsaw, a drill, a router and a finish sander**. With just these six tools, you will be amazed at what you can make, and how easy these alternative methods make it.

So grab some wood and give these methods a try. Trust me. If I can do it, you can do it better.

Basic Woodworking Tools Needed

POWER TOOLS	HAND TOOLS	WOOD BITS
Table Saw	Sanding Drums for Drill	1" Spade Bit
Belt Sander	Doweling Jig	2" Hole Saw
Jigsaw	Hammer and Nail Sets	
Drill	Square	
Router	Screwdrivers	
Finish Sander	Gluing Clamps	
	Pocket-Hole Drill Guide	
	Coping Saw	

alternative woodworking methods

I've developed some methods of making raised and flat-panel doors and cabinet sides. These methods have not failed me yet, so I invite you to try them.

Before you begin any of the projects in this book, I recommend that you build a gluing table. I constructed mine out of ¾" × 24" × 36" particleboard with 2" × 24" strips placed on edge so the clamps can be laid down inside.

RAISED PANEL SIDE OR DOOR

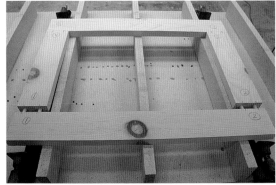

1 Use your doweling jig to dowel the outside frame of your raised panel side or door, glue the joints of the frame and clamp together firmly.

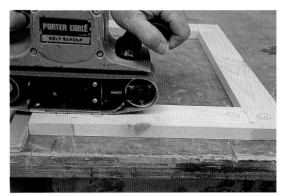

2 After the glue has dried, belt sand the joints smooth. Sand the rails first, then sand the stiles. This will eliminate the cross-grain scratches on the stiles.

3 After sanding, rout along the inside of the frame. I used a ¼" roundover bit; it creates a nice profile that's easy to sand.

4 Use your finish sander to sand out all of the scratches on the frame, and then do a little hand sanding. You can purchase a sanding pad at your local home-improvement store or use an old piece of carpet padding.

tip When woodworking, keep in mind that wood (like everything else) breathes. This means that the wood will expand and contract depending on whether it is winter or summer and/or with the level of humidity in the air. When making raised panels, be sure the insert will drop into its frame without any pressure, but do not leave a large gap; the expansion and contraction of small panels is relatively minimal.

tip When using a belt sander to sand the face frame or to sand other pieces in which the grain of one piece joins the grain of another piece in a T connection, sand the rails smooth across the grain of the stiles. Then sand the stiles . This will eliminate the cross-grain scratches. Finish sanding by hand or with a small finish sander.

RAISED PANEL SIDE OR DOOR *(continued)*

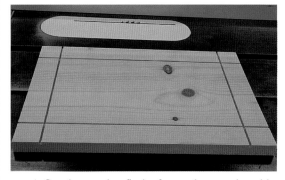

5 Cut the panel to fit the frame, then set the table saw blade to ⅛" deep and your fence to 1½" wide. Make the shoulder cuts for the profile.

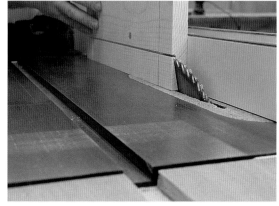

6 Set the table saw blade to a 10° angle and raise it to 1½" high. Make the second cut to create the profile on the panel.

7 With your finish sander, sand the panel to a smooth finish and final trim the panel with either a block plane or your finish sander so it will fit into the frame without any force. Sand carefully to avoid creating any gaps.

8 Cut your ¼" back panel the same size as the frame, apply glue to the back of the frame and attach the back panel with finish nails.

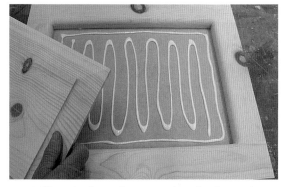

9 Turn the frame face up and apply glue to the inside of the back panel. Press the insert panel down firmly into the frame and onto the back panel. Apply weight on the insert panel until the glue is dry.

A TABLETOP OR FLAT-PANEL DOOR

1 There are many ways to glue wood together to form a larger panel. One quick and easy way is to use dowels about every 6" along the panel, apply glue to the edges of both panels and clamp them together.

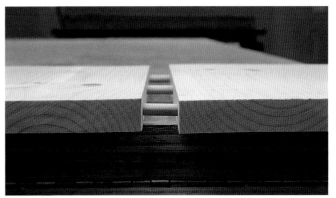

2 Take note of the end grain patterns of the wood; be sure that one pattern is opposed to the other. This ensures that the glued panel will remain relatively straight and flat.

3 After applying the glue, clamp the panel together using the gluing table. Wipe off any excess glue.

4 This panel trimming jig (a ¾" × 16" × 24" piece of plywood with a ¾" × 2" × 24" cleat at the back edge) runs against the table saw fence.

5 Glue two side pieces to your panel. Use dowels spaced about 6" apart.

6 Trim the panel to receive the front and back pieces.

7 Dowel and glue the front and back pieces to the panel.

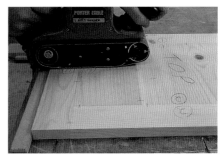

8 After the glue is dry and you have trimmed the edges, belt sand across the grain with a medium-grit belt, then sand with the grain using a fine-grit belt. Use a finish sander to complete the sanding.

end table

A great way to create some extra storage space in your living room is by building this end table. The tabletop opens, giving you room to store magazines, newspapers, that novel you've been reading and countless other items.

The top also has a fixed 8" portion on which to set a lamp, pictures, a coffee cup or other household necessities without interfering with the table's hinged top.

This end table is a lot of fun to make and is a great first project for trying out the skills you learned in "Alternative Woodworking Methods."

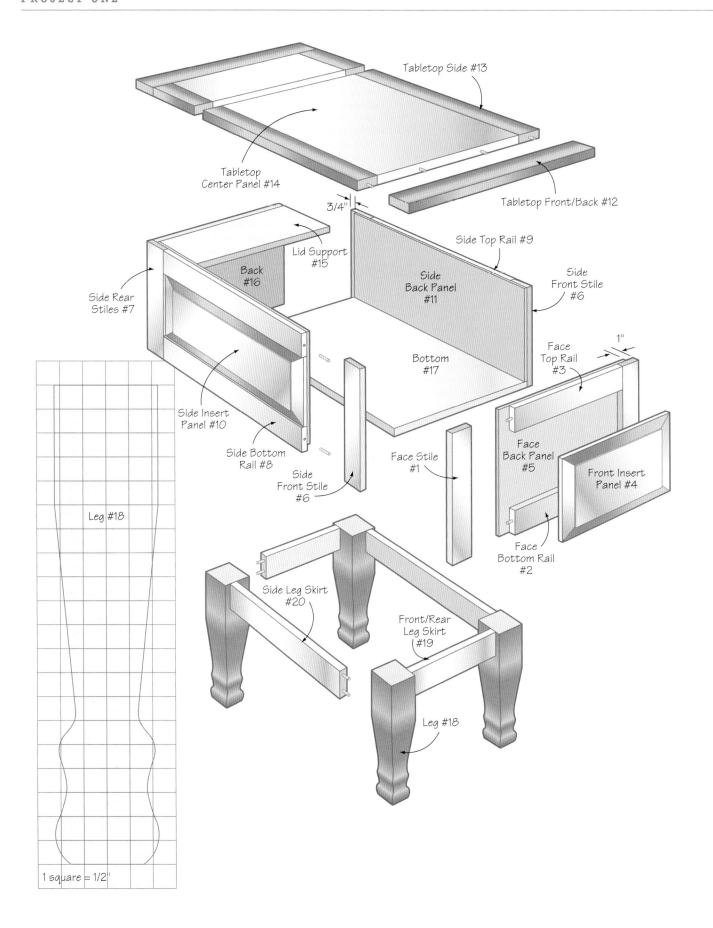

Tabletop Side #13

Tabletop Center Panel #14

Tabletop Front/Back #12

3/4"

Lid Support #15

Side Top Rail #9

Back #16

Side Back Panel #11

Side Front Stile #6

Side Rear Stiles #7

Bottom #17

Face Top Rail #3

1"

Face Back Panel #5

Front Insert Panel #4

Side Insert Panel #10

Side Bottom Rail #8

Side Front Stile #6

Face Stile #1

Face Bottom Rail #2

Leg #18

Side Leg Skirt #20

Front/Rear Leg Skirt #19

Leg #18

1 square = 1/2"

cutting list INCHES

REFERENCE	QUANTITY	PART	STOCK	THICKNESS	WIDTH	LENGTH	COMMENTS
1	2	Face Stiles	Pine	3/4	3	10	
2	1	Face Bottom Rail	Pine	3/4	2	8 3/4	
3	1	Face Top Rail	Pine	3/4	2 3/8	8 3/4	
4	1	Face Insert Panel	Pine	3/4	5 3/4	8 3/4	
5	1	Face Back Panel	Plywood	1/4	9 1/4	12 11/16	
6	2	Side Front Stiles	Pine	3/4	2 1/4	10	
7	2	Side Rear Stiles	Pine	3/4	3	10	
8	2	Side Bottom Rails	Pine	3/4	2	14	
9	2	Side Top Rails	Pine	3/4	2 3/8	14	
10	2	Side Insert Panels	Pine	3/4	5 3/4	14	
11	2	Side Back Panels	Plywood	1/4	9 1/4	18 7/16	
12	2	Tabletop Front & Back	Pine	1 1/4	3 1/8	17	
13	2	Tabletop Sides	Pine	1 1/4	3 1/8	16	
14	1	Tabletop Center Panel	Pine	1 1/4	10 3/4	16	
15	1	Lid Support	Pine	3/4	7 1/4	12 3/4	
16	1	Back	Plywood	3/4	10	13 1/4	
17	1	Bottom	Plywood	3/4	13 1/4	18 7/16	
18	4	Legs	Pine	2 1/4	2 1/4	10	A
19	2	Front & Rear Leg Skirts	Pine	3/4	2	8 5/8	
20	2	Side Leg Skirts	Pine	3/4	2	13 3/4	

*See "Alternative Woodworking Methods"

A: Glue together three 3/4" x 11" x 11 1/2" pieces

HARDWARE:

2- 1 1/2" x 2" butt hinges

cutting list MILLIMETERS

REFERENCE	QUANTITY	PART	STOCK	THICKNESS	WIDTH	LENGTH	COMMENTS
1	2	Face Stiles	Pine	19	76	254	
2	1	Face Bottom Rail	Pine	19	51	222	
3	1	Face Top Rail	Pine	19	61	222	
4	1	Face Insert Panel	Pine	19	146	222	
5	1	Face Back Panel	Plywood	6	235	323	
6	2	Side Front Stiles	Pine	19	57	254	
7	2	Side Rear Stiles	Pine	19	76	254	
8	2	Side Bottom Rails	Pine	19	51	356	
9	2	Side Top Rails	Pine	19	61	356	
10	2	Side Insert Panels	Pine	19	146	356	
11	2	Side Back Panels	Plywood	6	235	468	
12	2	Tabletop Front & Back	Pine	31	79	432	
13	2	Tabletop Sides	Pine	31	79	406	
14	1	Tabletop Center Panel	Pine	31	273	406	
15	1	Lid Support	Pine	19	184	324	
16	1	Back	Plywood	19	254	336	
17	1	Bottom	Plywood	19	336	468	
18	4	Legs	Pine	57	57	254	A
19	2	Front & Rear Leg Skirts	Pine	19	51	219	
20	2	Side Leg Skirts	Pine	19	51	349	

*See "Alternative Woodworking Methods"

A: Glue together three 19mm x 279 mm x 292 mm pieces

HARDWARE:

2- 38mm x 51mm butt hinges

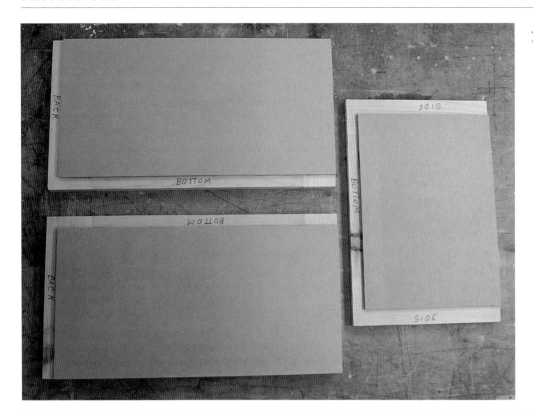

1 When you attach the ¼" back panels to the raised-panels (see "Alternative Woodworking Methods" on page 9-10), notice that there is a right side, a left side and a front. The back panel (not shown) is ¾" plywood.

2 Attach the front and back to the side pieces with glue and finish nails.

3 Turn the cabinet upside down and attach the ¾" bottom to the sides, back and front with glue and finish nails.

4   Using a scrap piece of wood, spread glue evenly on the leg blank parts.

5   After you've applied glue to all three pieces, clamp them together firmly.

6   Use your miter gauge to cut the leg blank to length, then use your table saw to rip them into four individual legs.

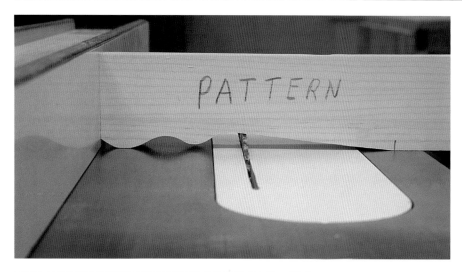

7   Use your jigsaw to cut a leg design pattern on a scrap piece of wood. The top 2½" must remain square.

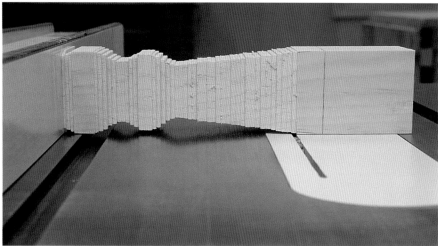

8   Begin at the foot of the leg. Set your table saw blade depth so the top of the blade just touches the pattern. Make a cut on all four sides of each leg. Then move your fence the thickness of your saw blade and adjust the blade depth to match the pattern in the new position. Now make the new cuts. Continue repeating this process until all four legs are cut.

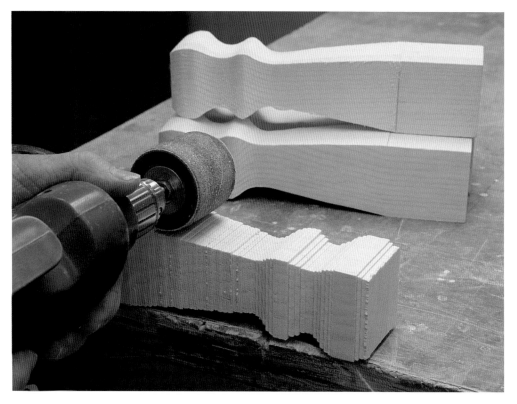

9   Attach a sanding drum to your drill and sand out all of the saw marks on each leg. Finish sand by hand.

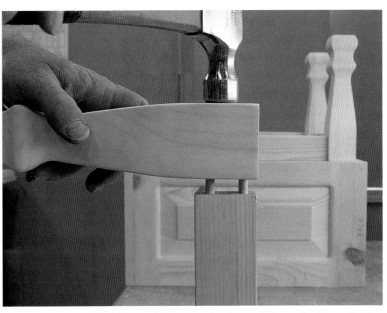

10 Mark the positions of the dowels on the legs and on the leg skirts. The skirts sit ⅜" inside the outside edge of the legs.

11 Dowel all of the legs and skirts, apply glue and clamp the leg and skirt assembly together.

12 After you have completed the leg-and-skirt assembly, turn over the end-table box and place the leg assembly on the bottom. Center the assembly on the box and trace around it.

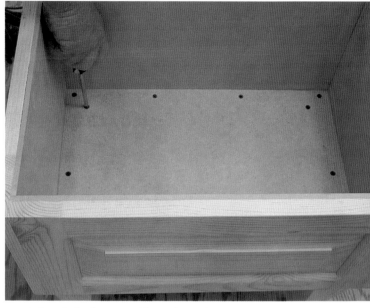

13 Drill holes in the bottom of the end table so you can attach the leg assembly.

14 Attach the leg assembly to the end table with 1½" screws.

15 Use a ¼" roundover bit to round the edges of the end table.

16 After making the top (see page 11), add thickness to it by attaching 1" × ³⁄₈" strips to the bottom edges. Be sure to keep the nails away from the edges that you'll be rounding with the router.

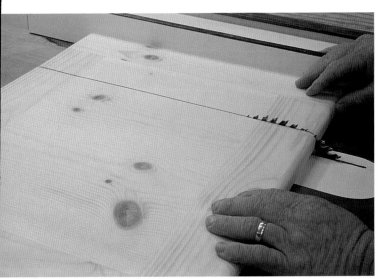

17 After you've rounded over the top and bottom edges of the top with your router, finish sand it. Then set your table saw fence to 8" and cut the top in two. Now glue the lid support piece in place inside the cabinet.

18 Attach the 8" portion of the top to the end table with 1¼" screws driven up through the lid support. Attach the other part of the top to the 8" section with 2 flat hinges. This lid overlaps the front of the cabinet which makes it easy to open.

curio cabinet
with bottom storage

Most homes have a few corners that are just sort of there—corners that are not utilized in any substantial way. A corner curio cabinet can make excellent use of this space.

With the addition of glass doors, this cabinet will give you a place to display your precious family mementos, or anything else that tickles your fancy.

The cabinet has two drawers in the lower part that will come in handy for additional storage. This project is a great addition to any home.

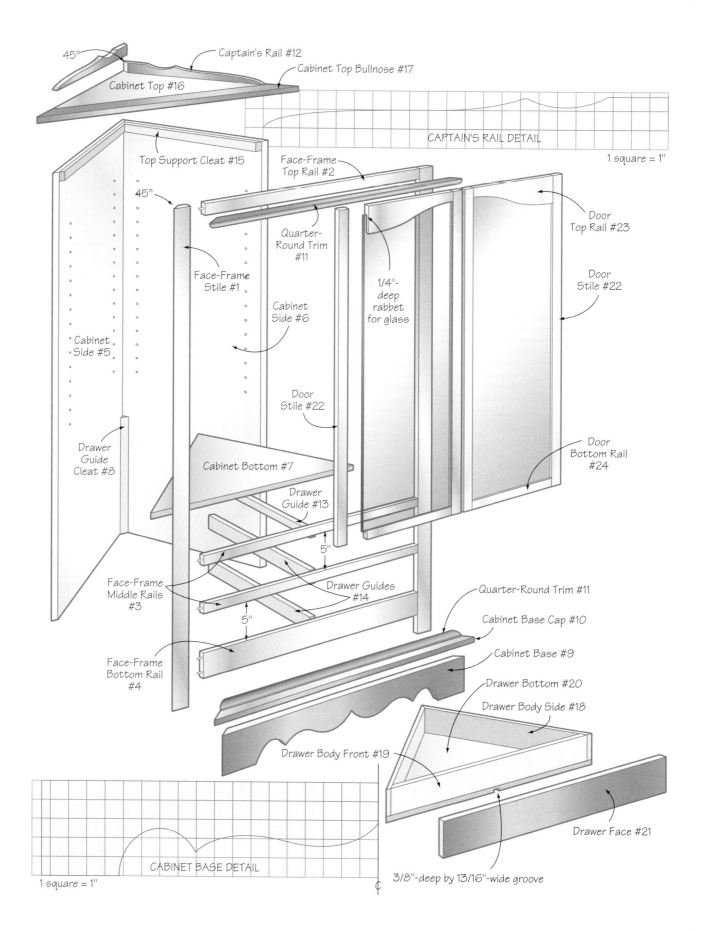

45°
Captain's Rail #12
Cabinet Top Bullnose #17
Cabinet Top #16
CAPTAIN'S RAIL DETAIL
1 square = 1"

Top Support Cleat #15
Face-Frame Top Rail #2
Door Top Rail #23

45°
Quarter-Round Trim #11
Face-Frame Stile #1
Cabinet Side #6
1/4"-deep rabbet for glass
Door Stile #22

Cabinet Side #5
Door Stile #22
Door Bottom Rail #24

Drawer Guide Cleat #8
Cabinet Bottom #7
Drawer Guide #13

5"

Face-Frame Middle Rails #3
Drawer Guides #14
Quarter-Round Trim #11
Cabinet Base Cap #10
Cabinet Base #9

5"
Drawer Bottom #20
Drawer Body Side #18

Face-Frame Bottom Rail #4
Drawer Body Front #19
Drawer Face #21

CABINET BASE DETAIL
1 square = 1"
3/8"-deep by 13/16"-wide groove

cutting list INCHES

REFERENCE	QUANTITY	PART	STOCK	THICKNESS	WIDTH	LENGTH	COMMENTS
1	2	Face-Frame Stiles	Oak	$3/4$	$2^{1}/_2$	$61^{1}/_2$	
2	1	Face-Frame Top Rail	Oak	$3/4$	$1^{3}/_4$	29	
3	2	Face-Frame Middle Rails	Oak	$3/4$	$1^{1}/_2$	29	
4	1	Face-Frame Bottom Rail	Oak	$3/4$	4	29	
5	1	Cabinet Side	Oak Ply.*	$3/4$	$22^{3}/_4$	$61^{1}/_2$	F
6	1	Cabinet Side	Oak Ply.	$3/4$	22	$61^{1}/_2$	
7	1	Cabinet Bottom	Oak Ply.	$3/4$	16	32	E
8	1	Drawer Guide Cleat	Any	$3/4$	$3/4$	20	C
9	1	Cabinet Base	Oak	$3/4$	5	37	A, D
10	1	Cabinet Base Cap	Oak	$3/4$	$1^{1}/_4$	37	A
11	2	Quarter-Round Trim	Oak	$1/2$	$1/2$	37	A
12	2	Captain's Rails	Oak	$3/8$	$1^{3}/_4$	23	B, D
13	1	Drawer Guide	Any	$3/4$	$1^{1}/_8$	16	
14	2	Drawer Guides	Any	$3/4$	$2^{1}/_4$	16	
15	2	Top Support Cleats	Oak	$3/4$	$1^{1}/_2$	22	A
16	1	Cabinet Top	Oak Ply.	$3/4$	18	35	E
17	1	Cabinet Top Bullnose	Oak	$3/4$	1	37	A
18	4	Drawer Body Sides	Melamine	$1/2$	$4^{1}/_2$	$20^{1}/_2$	A
19	2	Drawer Body Fronts	Melamine	$1/2$	$3^{3}/_4$	$27^{1}/_2$	A
20	2	Drawer Bottoms	Melamine	$3/4$	14	28	
21	2	Drawer Faces	Oak	$3/4$	$5^{1}/_2$	$29^{1}/_2$	
22	4	Door Stiles	Oak	$3/4$	$1^{3}/_4$	$41^{3}/_8$	D
23	2	Door Top Rails	Oak	$3/4$	4	$11^{1}/_4$	
24	2	Door Bottom Rails	Oak	$3/4$	$1^{3}/_4$	$11^{1}/_4$	

*Plywood

A: 45° cuts on both ends

B: 45° cut on one end

C: Triangle cleat

D: Cut to design profile

E: Layout on template before cutting out

F: 45° cut on one long edge

HARDWARE:

12' of $5/8$"-wide edge banding tape to match color of melamine

2 - $1/8$" door-glass pieces, cut to fit

3 - $1/4$" tempered glass shelves, cut to fit

12 - $1/4$" shelf support clips

4 full-overlay, self-closing, face frame hinges

2 door knobs

2 drawer pulls

cutting list MILLIMETERS

REFERENCE	QUANTITY	PART	STOCK	THICKNESS	WIDTH	LENGTH	COMMENTS
1	2	Face-Frame Stiles	Oak	19	64	1562	
2	1	Face-Frame Top Rail	Oak	19	45	737	
3	2	Face-Frame Middle Rails	Oak	19	38	737	
4	1	Face-Frame Bottom Rail	Oak	19	102	737	
5	1	Cabinet Side	Oak Ply.*	19	578	1562	F
6	1	Cabinet Side	Oak Ply.	19	559	1562	
7	1	Cabinet Bottom	Oak Ply.	19	406	813	E
8	1	Drawer Guide Cleat	Any	19	19	508	C
9	1	Cabinet Base	Oak	19	127	940	A, D
10	1	Cabinet Base Cap	Oak	19	32	940	A
11	2	Quarter-Round Trim	Oak	13	13	940	A
12	2	Captain's Rails	Oak	10	45	584	B, D
13	1	Drawer Guide	Any	19	29	406	
14	2	Drawer Guides	Any	19	32	406	
15	2	Top Support Cleats	Oak	19	38	559	A
16	1	Cabinet Top	Oak Ply.	19	457	889	E
17	1	Cabinet Top Bullnose	Oak	19	25	940	A
18	4	Drawer Body Sides	Melamine	13	115	521	A
19	2	Drawer Body Fronts	Melamine	13	95	699	A
20	2	Drawer Bottoms	Melamine	19	356	711	
21	2	Drawer Faces	Oak	19	140	750	
22	4	Door Stiles	Oak	19	45	1051	D
23	2	Door Top Rails	Oak	19	102	285	
24	2	Door Bottom Rails	Oak	19	45	285	

*Plywood

A: 45° cuts on both ends

B: 45° cut on one end

C: Triangle cleat

D: Cut to design profile

E: Layout on template before cutting out

F: 45° cut on one long edge

HARDWARE:

3.7m of 16mm-wide edge banding tape to match color of melamine

2 - 3 mm door-glass pieces, cut to fit

3 - 6 mm tempered glass shelves, cut to fit

12 - 6 mm shelf support clips

4 full-overlay, self-closing, face frame hinges

2 door knobs

2 drawer pulls

1   Use a scrap piece of plywood or cardboard to make a template of the footprint of the curio cabinet. Use the measurements given in the cutting list, or use your own measurements for a custom size.

2   Use the template to trace out the top of the cabinet. The top will sit on top of the face frame and sides and will be the full, finished size of the curio cabinet. Deduct ¾" from each side and face of the template, and trace an inside shelf.

3 Use the sliding table jig (see page 11, step #4) to cut out the top and inside shelves on a 45° angle. If you don't feel comfortable doing this operation, rough cut the top using a jigsaw. Then, clamp a straight edge along the line and trim it smooth with a straight cutting bit and a router. Then, glue a 1" × ¾" piece to the front edge of the top to conceal the veneer's end grain.

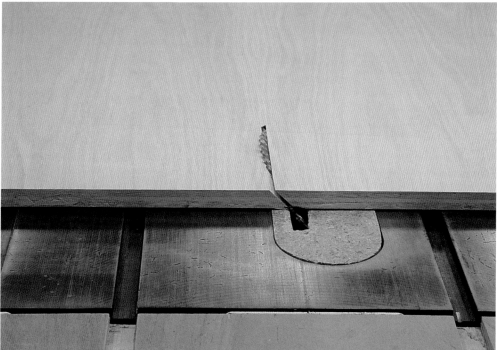

4 Cut a 45° angle on the fronts of the side pieces. The face frame will be attached to this edge.

5 Assemble the face frame using dowels. After you've assembled the frame, lay it face down and cut a 45° angle on each outside edge of the stiles. The inside width of the frame (angle to angle) will be about ½" wider than the cabinet's face.

6 Lay the face frame on the side pieces. Be sure it is a flush fit top to bottom, then trace on the side where you will attach the shelf.

7 Assemble the the sides with glue and screws at their back edges. (When assembling the side pieces, notice that one is ¾" longer than the other, so they must overlap correctly in order to form a perfect triangle.) Then, glue and screw the shelf into place. Prop up the assembly for attaching the face frame.

8   Apply glue to both front edges of the side panels and the face of the shelf, then, lay the face frame on the assembly and attach it with nails.

9   Cut a triangle cleat and glue it in the back corner. This will make it easier for you to install the drawer guides.

10   As you install the drawer guides, note that they protrude ⅜" above and ⅜" below the drawer rail. Check that they are square to the cabinet's face.

11 Make a drilling jig from a scrap piece of wood with ¼" holes every 2" on center. Use the jig to drill the holes ⅜"-deep for the shelf support clips. (Note the stop block on the drill bit. This will stop the drill at the proper hole depth and prevent you from drilling through the cabinet side.)

12 Install the top support cleats. Then, attach the top using 1¼" screws.

13 Install the ½" quarter-round trim with the ends cut on 45° angles to match the cabinet. Attach with finish nails.

14 With your jigsaw, cut the scroll design (see the technical drawing for a pattern) into the cabinet base piece. Then, cut the ends on 45° angles to match the cabinet's width.

15 Attach the cabinet base to the face frame with nails. Then, cut and attach the cabinet base cap to the cabinet base. Finally, attach the ½" quarter-round trim to the top of the base cap.

16 Cut the profile on the captain's rails and sand. Attach the moulding to the top of the cabinet's back edges (see technical illustration). Apply glue and hold it in place with masking tape.

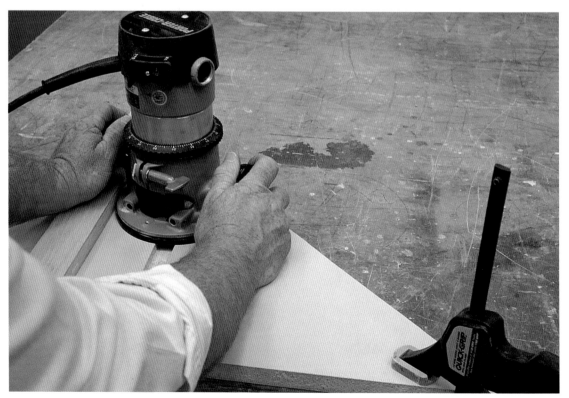

tip If you plan to place your curio cabinet on a carpeted area, you might want to cut ½" off the bottom of the cabinet in the back. Taper this cut to nothing at the front base. This will make the cabinet more stable on the carpeted surface.

17 Cut out the drawer bottoms like you did the cabinet top (see step 4). Then rout a $^{13}/_{16}$"-wide by $^3/_8$"-deep groove for the drawer guide in the drawer bottoms.

18 Using contact cement, apply white edge-banding to the top edges of the drawer sides and front. After trimming the edge banding, assemble the drawer body using glue and nails. Then, center the drawer face on the body and attach it with 1" screws.

19 Set your router to a depth of ¼" (using a straight cutting bit) and rout the inside of the door to accept a glass panel. (It is much cheaper to rout the door to fit a rectangular piece of glass than to have a piece of glass cut to fit a curved-top door.) Turn the door over and rout the inside and outside edges of the front with a ¼" roundover bit. After the finish has been applied to the cabinet, apply a small bead of clear silicone adhesive in the rabbets on the inside of the doors. Then, set the glass into the rabbets and *gently* seat the glass in the silicone. Let the silicone setup before installing the doors on the cabinet.

20 Install the doors with an attractive self-closing cabinet hinge. Remove the doors prior to applying the finish of your choice.

dining room table

The dining room is traditionally the place where families can sit down and talk about their day over the evening meal. Friends and family can get together and play a friendly board game there. So why not make a special table for that special place? This functional and beautiful table would go perfectly in that family gathering place. It will seat six people comfortably. It has two drawers on each side for placemats, tablecloths or maybe even that board game.

This table project is a lot of fun to build, but remember that old saying: Patience is a virtue! The legs are a bit time-consuming to make, so take your time.

Bon appétit!

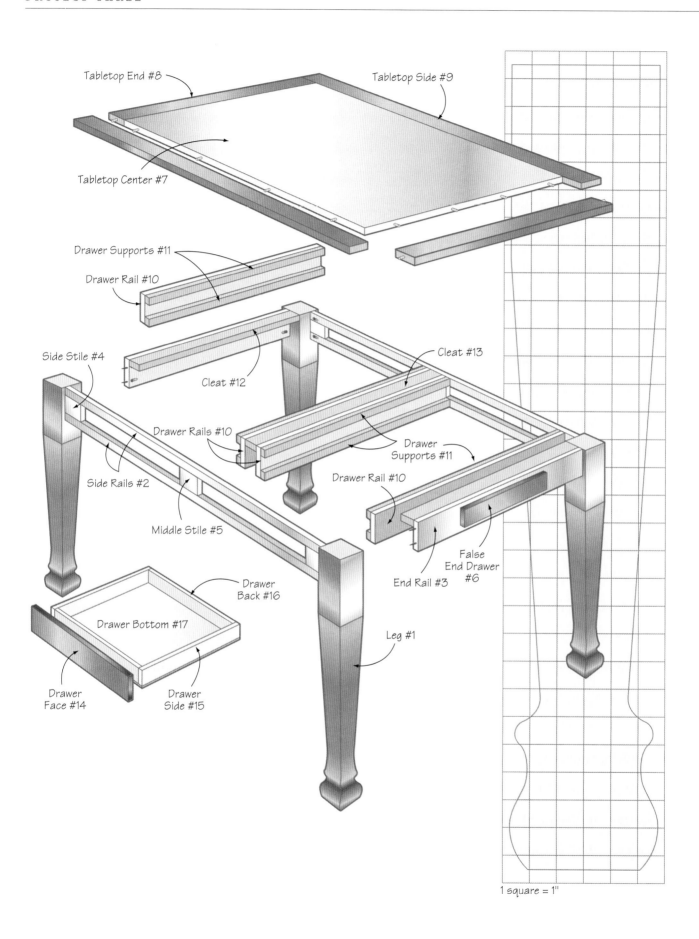

Tabletop End #8

Tabletop Side #9

Tabletop Center #7

Drawer Supports #11

Drawer Rail #10

Side Stile #4

Cleat #12

Cleat #13

Drawer Rails #10

Drawer Supports #11

Side Rails #2

Drawer Rail #10

Middle Stile #5

Drawer Back #16

Drawer Bottom #17

End Rail #3

False End Drawer #6

Leg #1

Drawer Face #14

Drawer Side #15

1 square = 1"

cutting list **INCHES**

REFERENCE	QUANTITY	PART	STOCK	THICKNESS	WIDTH	LENGTH	COMMENTS
1	4	Legs	Oak	$5^1/_2$	$5^1/_2$	$29^1/_2$	
2	4	Side Rails	Oak	$^3/_4$	1	$52^1/_2$	
3	2	End Rails	Oak	$^3/_4$	$4^1/_2$	$29^1/_8$	
4	4	Side Stiles	Oak	$^3/_4$	3	$2^1/_2$	
5	2	Middle Stiles	Oak	$^3/_4$	$3^1/_2$	$2^1/_2$	
6	2	False End Drawers	Oak	$^3/_4$	3	24	
7	1	Tabletop Center	Oak Ply	$^3/_4$	$36^1/_4$	$59^1/_4$	
8	2	Tabletop Ends	Oak	$1^1/_8$	$3^1/_2$	$36^1/_4$	
9	2	Tabletop Sides	Oak	$1^1/_8$	$3^1/_2$	$66^1/_4$	
10	4	Drawer Rails	Plywood	$^3/_4$	$4^1/_2$	37	
11	8	Drawer Supports	Plywood	$^3/_4$	1	37	
12	2	Cleats	Plywood	$^3/_4$	$2^1/_2$	$29^1/_8$	
13	1	Cleat	Plywood	$^3/_4$	2	37	
14	4	Drawer Faces	Oak	$^3/_4$	3	$22^1/_2$	
15	8	Drawer Sides	Melamine	$^1/_2$	2	19	
16	8	Drawer Fronts and Backs	Melamine	$^1/_2$	2	$20^3/_8$	
17	4	Drawer Bottoms	Melamine	$^1/_4$	19	$21^3/_8$	

HARDWARE:

30' of $^5/_8$"-wide edge tape to match color of melamine PB

6 drawer pulls

cutting list **MILLIMETERS**

REFERENCE	QUANTITY	PART	STOCK	THICKNESS	WIDTH	LENGTH	COMMENTS
1	4	Legs	Oak	140	140	750	
2	4	Side Rails	Oak	19	25	1334	
3	2	End Rails	Oak	19	115	740	
4	4	Side Stiles	Oak	19	76	64	
5	2	Middle Stiles	Oak	19	89	64	
6	2	False End Drawers	Oak	19	76	610	
7	1	Tabletop Center	Oak Ply	19	920	1505	
8	2	Tabletop Ends	Oak	29	89	920	
9	2	Tabletop Sides	Oak	29	89	1682	
10	4	Drawer Rails	Plywood	19	115	940	
11	8	Drawer Supports	Plywood	19	25	940	
12	2	Cleats	Plywood	19	64	740	
13	1	Cleat	Plywood	19	51	940	
14	4	Drawer Faces	Oak	19	76	572	
15	8	Drawer Sides	Melamine	13	51	483	
16	8	Drawer Fronts & Backs	Melamine	13	51	518	
17	4	Drawer Bottoms	Melamine	6	483	543	

HARDWARE:

9m of 16mm-wide edge tape to match color of melamine PB

6 drawer pulls

1 For each of the four legs, glue enough pieces of oak together to make four 5¾" × 5¾" × 30½" blanks. Sand off the glue joints on one side with a belt sander, making sure the blanks have two adjacent sides that are square.

2 Keep the two square sides to the fence on your table saw and cut the leg to 5½" × 5½".

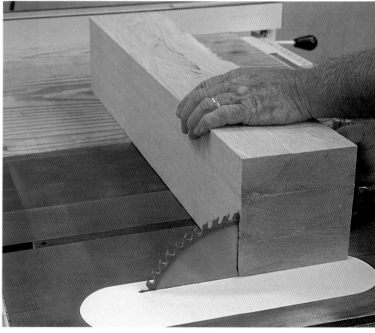

3 Cut one end of each leg blank square. (Make this cut in two passes by flipping the leg over.) Mark for length and cut the other end square to the final length.

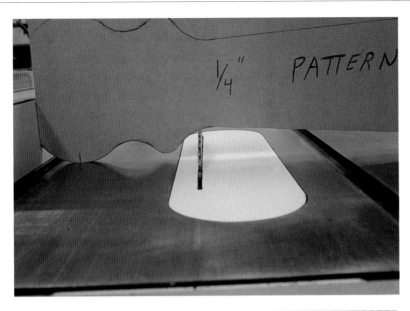

4 Draw a leg design on a piece of scrap wood and cut it out using a jigsaw. The top 7½" on the leg must remain square.

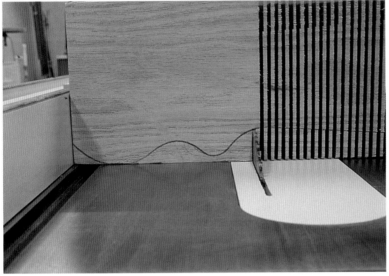

5 Set your saw blade so it just touches the pattern at the 7½" mark. Then make a cut on all four sides of each leg. Move your fence in ¼" increments and adjust the blade depth to match the pattern in the new position. Make another cut on all four sides of each leg. Repeat this process until you've cut all four legs.

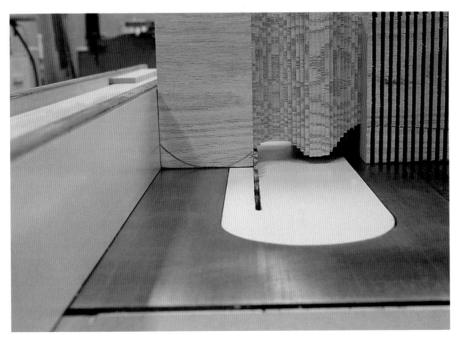

6 When you reach the part of the leg where there is more curvature, move the fence in ⅛" increments.

7 | Use a chisel to cut away the scrap wood.

8 | Sand off all saw marks on the lower end of the legs using your drill and a sanding drum

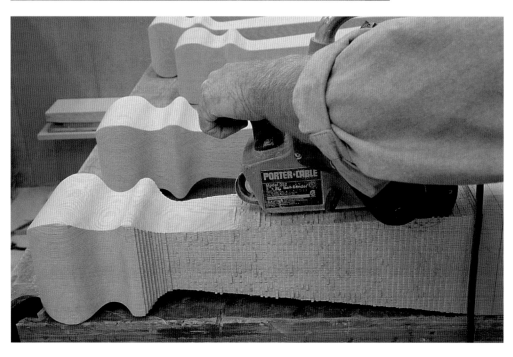

9 | Sand off all saw and chisel marks on the upper portion of the legs using your belt sander.

10 Refer to the technical art and assemble the side rails for the table using glue and clamps. Use spacers between the side stiles and the middle stile to ensure the proper drawing opening is achieved. After the glue has set up, use your drill and a pocket-hole drilling jig to drill pocket-holes for the screws that will fasten the rails to the table legs.

11 Screw the side and end rails to all four legs. Use a ¾"- square spacer-block clamped into place to hold the rail in position against the table leg. Attach the false drawer fronts and cleats to the two end rails at this time.

12 Assemble your drawer track rails. Note that the drawer track rails go all the way across the table. (The drawers opposite each other use the same rails.) Be sure the tracks are flush on the top, bottom and sides as you assemble them. Attach the rails to the aprons with glue and nails.

13 Place the table frame upside down on your workbench. Use a router with a ½" roundover bit to rout the bottoms of the side rails.

14 Note that the router will not go all the way to the end of the rail—it will hit the leg. This is ok. I left this part of the rail square going into the leg because I thought it looked nice.

tip When you sand a tabletop made with veneer plywood, be sure to use extreme care so you don't sand through the veneer at the hardwood joint. (See photo #15.)

15 See "Alternative Woodworking Methods" on page 11 for tabletop construction. After you've assembled the tabletop and used a ½" roundover bit on the top and bottom edges, finish sand with your finish sander.

16 Drill pocket holes into the table aprons and attach the tabletop to the base. Assemble the drawers and install the 2 false drawer ends. Stain and finish the table and you're done!

grandfather clock
with secret storage

A grandfather clock is a warm and welcome addition to anyone's home, but unfortunately, also very expensive to buy. The grandfather clock in this project is very inexpensive, since you can build it yourself, but it's still a masterpiece.

The display case in the center is a perfect place to store those precious family heirlooms, or it could also be used as a bookcase.

The bottom of the clock opens for additional storage. Another special feature of this clock is a secret storage shelf, located above the clock mechanism, in which you could store valuable jewelry or even that million dollars you might have just sitting around.

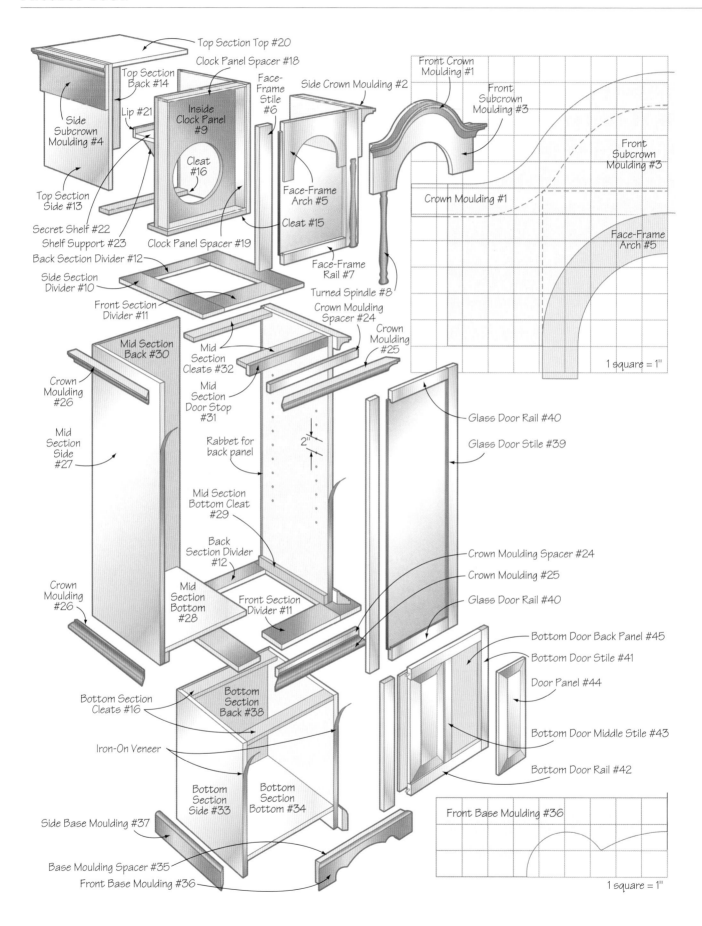

Top Section Top #20
Clock Panel Spacer #18
Top Section Back #14
Face-Frame Stile #6
Side Crown Moulding #2
Front Crown Moulding #1
Front Subcrown Moulding #3
Inside Clock Panel #9
Lip #21
Side Subcrown Moulding #4
Cleat #16
Front Subcrown Moulding #3
Crown Moulding #1
Top Section Side #13
Face-Frame Arch #5
Face-Frame Arch #5
Secret Shelf #22
Cleat #15
Shelf Support #23
Clock Panel Spacer #19
Back Section Divider #12
Side Section Divider #10
Face-Frame Rail #7
Front Section Divider #11
Turned Spindle #8
Crown Moulding Spacer #24
1 square = 1"
Mid Section Back #30
Crown Moulding #25
Mid Section Cleats #32
Crown Moulding #26
Mid Section Door Stop #31
Glass Door Rail #40
Mid Section Side #27
Glass Door Stile #39
Rabbet for back panel
2"
Mid Section Bottom Cleat #29
Back Section Divider #12
Crown Moulding Spacer #24
Crown Moulding #25
Crown Moulding #26
Mid Section Bottom #28
Front Section Divider #11
Glass Door Rail #40
Bottom Door Back Panel #45
Bottom Door Stile #41
Bottom Section Cleats #16
Bottom Section Back #38
Door Panel #44
Iron-On Veneer
Bottom Door Middle Stile #43
Bottom Section Side #33
Bottom Section Bottom #34
Bottom Door Rail #42
Side Base Moulding #37
Front Base Moulding #36
Base Moulding Spacer #35
Front Base Moulding #36
1 square = 1"

46

cutting list **INCHES**

REFERENCE	QUANTITY	PART	STOCK	THICKNESS	WIDTH	LENGTH	COMMENTS
1	1	Front Crown Moulding	QSWO*	1¼	6	20	Cut to design; trim to fit
2	2	Side Crown Moulding	QSWO	1¼	1¼	15	Trim to fit
3	1	Front Subcrown Moulding	QSWO	¾	10½	17	Cut to design; trim to fit
4	2	Side Subcrown Moulding	QSWO	¾	6	14	Trim to fit
5	1	Face-Frame Arch	QSWO	¾	7⅛	9¾	Cut to design
6	2	Face-Frame Stiles	QSWO	¾	2¼	17¾	
7	1	Face-Frame Rail	QSWO	¾	1½	9¾	
8	2	Turned Spindles	QSWO	½	1⅛	11¾	Buy one 36" stair spindle
9	1	Inside Clock Panel	QSWO	¾	12¹¹⁄₁₆	16⅛	
10	4	Side Section Dividers	QSWO	¾	3	12¾	
11	2	Front Section Dividers	QSWO	¾	4¾	9¾	
12	2	Back Section Dividers	QSWO	¾	1½	9¾	
13	2	Top Section Sides	Oak Ply.**	¾	11¼	17¾	
14	1	Top Section Back	Oak Ply.	¼	13½	17¾	
15	1	Top Section Cleat	Any	¾	3	12¾	
16	2	Top & Bottom Section Cleats	Oak	¾	1½	12¾	
17	1	Clock Panel Bottom Spacer	Oak Ply.	¼	1½	11¼	
18	1	Clock Panel Top Spacer	Oak Ply.	¾	1½	11¼	
19	2	Clock Panel Side Spacers	Oak Ply.	¾	1½	16¼	
20	1	Top Section Top	Oak Ply.	¾	11	12¾	
21	1	Secret Shelf Lip	Any	¼	1⅛	12¹¹⁄₁₆	
22	1	Secret Shelf	Any	¾	4	12¹¹⁄₁₆	
23	2	Secret Shelf Supports	Any	¾	3	3	Cut into triangles
24	2	Crown Moulding Spacers	QSWO	¾	1¼	12	
25	2	Crown Moulding Faces	QSWO	1¼	1¼	16	Trim to fit
26	4	Crown Moulding Sides	QSWO	1¼	1¼	13	Trim to fit
27	2	Middle Section Sides	Oak Ply.	¾	9¾	34⅛	
28	1	Middle Section Bottom	Oak Ply.	¾	9½	10½	
29	2	Middle Section Bottom Cleats	Any	¾	⅞	9½	
30	1	Middle Section Back	Oak Ply.	¼	11¼	34⅛	
31	1	Middle Section Doorstop	QSWO	¾	1⅝	10½	
32	2	Middle Section Cleats	Any	¾	1½	10½	
33	2	Bottom Section Sides	Oak Ply.	¾	11¼	20⅛	
34	1	Bottom Section Bottom	Oak Ply.	¾	11	12¾	
35	1	Base Moulding Spacer	QSWO	¾	3	14¼	
36	1	Base Moulding Front	QSWO	¾	3	18	Cut to design; trim to fit
37	2	Base Moulding Sides	QSWO	¾	3	14	Trim to fit
38	1	Bottom Section Back	Oak Ply.	¼	13½	20⅛	
39	2	Glass Door Stiles	QSWO	¾	1½	31½	
40	2	Glass Door Rails	QSWO	¾	1½	9	
41	2	Bottom Door Stiles	QSWO	¾	1½	16⅞	
42	2	Bottom Door Rails	QSWO	¾	1½	11¼	
43	1	Bottom Door Middle Stile	QSWO	¾	1½	13⅞	
44	2	Bottom Door Panels	QSWO	¾	4⅞	13⅞	
45	1	Bottom Door Back Panel	Oak Ply.	¼	12¼	15	

HARDWARE:

10' of ¹³⁄₁₆ - ⅞"-wide oak iron-on edge banding
2 tempered glass shelves ¼" x 9¼" x 10½"
1 door glass ⅛" x 9¾" x 29½"
8 - ¼" shelf supports
4 door hinges
2 door knobs
1 battery clock 8" diameter
2 magnetic latches

*Quartersawn White Oak
**Plywood
***A great reference book for new techniques/ hardware is *Fast & Easy Techniques for Building Modern Cabinetry* by Danny Proulx (Popular Woodworking Books).

cutting list MILLIMETERS

REFERENCE	QUANTITY	PART	STOCK	THICKNESS	WIDTH	LENGTH	COMMENTS
1	1	Front Crown Moulding	QSWO*	32	152	508	Cut to design; trim to fit
2	2	Side Crown Moulding	QSWO	32	32	381	Trim to fit
3	1	Front Subcrown Moulding	QSWO	19	267	432	Cut to design; trim to fit
4	2	Side Subcrown Moulding	QSWO	19	152	356	Trim to fit
5	1	Face-Frame Arch	QSWO	19	181	248	Cut to design
6	2	Face-Frame Stiles	QSWO	19	57	451	
7	1	Face-Frame Rail	QSWO	19	38	248	
8	2	Turned Spindles	QSWO	13	29	298	Buy one 1m stair spindle
9	1	Inside Clock Panel	QSWO	19	323	411	
10	4	Side Section Dividers	QSWO	19	76	311	
11	2	Front Section Dividers	QSWO	19	121	248	
12	2	Back Section Dividers	QSWO	19	38	248	
13	2	Top Section Sides	Oak Ply.**	19	32	451	
14	1	Top Section Back	Oak Ply.	6	343	451	
15	1	Top Section Cleat	Any	19	76	311	
16	2	Top & Bottom Section Cleats	Oak	19	38	311	
17	1	Clock Panel Bottom Spacer	Oak Ply.	6	38	285	
18	1	Clock Panel Top Spacer	Oak Ply.	19	38	285	
19	2	Clock Panel Side Spacers	Oak Ply.	19	38	412	
20	1	Top Section Top	Oak Ply.	19	279	324	
21	1	Secret Shelf Lip	Any	6	29	323	
22	1	Secret Shelf	Any	19	102	323	
23	2	Secret Shelf Supports	Any	19	76	76	Cut into triangles
24	2	Crown Moulding Spacers	QSWO	19	32	305	
25	2	Crown Moulding Faces	QSWO	32	32	406	Trim to fit
26	4	Crown Moulding Sides	QSWO	32	32	330	Trim to fit
27	2	Middle Section Sides	Oak Ply.	19	248	867	
28	1	Middle Section Bottom	Oak Ply.	19	242	267	
29	2	Middle Section Bottom Cleats	Any	19	22	242	
30	1	Middle Section Back	Oak Ply.	6	285	867	
31	1	Middle Section Doorstop	QSWO	19	41	267	
32	2	Middle Section Cleats	Any	19	38	267	
33	2	Bottom Section Sides	Oak Ply.	19	285	511	
34	1	Bottom Section Bottom	Oak Ply.	19	279	324	
35	1	Base Moulding Spacer	QSWO	19	76	362	
36	1	Base Moulding Front	QSWO	19	76	457	Cut to design; trim to fit
37	2	Base Moulding Sides	QSWO	19	76	356	Trim to fit
38	1	Bottom Section Back	Oak Ply.	6	343	511	
39	2	Glass Door Stiles	QSWO	19	38	800	
40	2	Glass Door Rails	QSWO	19	38	229	
41	2	Bottom Door Stiles	QSWO	19	38	428	
42	2	Bottom Door Rails	QSWO	19	38	285	
43	1	Bottom Door Middle Stile	QSWO	19	38	352	
44	2	Bottom Door Panels	QSWO	19	124	352	
45	1	Bottom Door Back Panel	Oak Ply.	6	311	381	

HARDWARE:

3m of 21-22mm-wide oak iron-on edge banding

2 tempered glass shelves 6 x 209 x 267 mm

1 door glass 3 x 209 x 750 mm

8 – 6 mm shelf supports

4 door hinges

2 door knobs

1 battery clock 203 mm diameter

2 magnetic latches

*Quartersawn White Oak

**Plywood

***A great reference book for new techniques/ hardware is *Fast & Easy Techniques for Building Modern Cabinetry* by Danny Proulx (Popular Woodworking Books).

1 Purchase an inexpensive battery-powered wall clock from any home-improvement or retail store. Look for something that can be removed from its frame and has an appearance that fits the look of a grandfather clock.

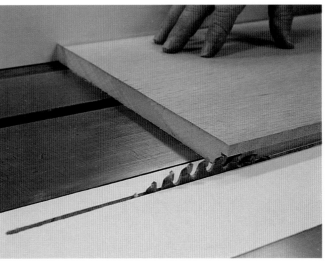

2 Cut the sides of the midsection and the face according to the cutting list, then cut a ¼" × ¼" rabbet in the back of the clock sides. This rabbet will receive the ¼" back panel.

3 Apply the edge banding to the midsection and the base section front edges to cover the plywood edges. Use iron-on banding material that matches the wood you are using to build the clock.

4 Using a drilling jig made out of scrap material, drill ¼" shelf clip holes 2" apart and ⅜"-deep on the inside midsection.

5   Rout a ¼" roundover detail on the tops and bottoms of the sides and front of the section dividers. After making the roundover, assemble the midsection. Then screw one of the dividers to the bottom of the midsection.

6   Assemble the base section in the same fashion as the mid-section. Screw the base section to the midsection divider.

7   Make a template for the front base moulding profile per the technical drawing, trace it on the base, cut and sand. (You may choose to not use the profile as shown in the photo.) Nail the baseboard onto the base of the clock. Note the ¾" spacer block that holds the baseboard out from the front of the base. This puts the baseboard out in front of the face of the door.

8   Assemble the face of the top section. Cut the arch in the face panel, and sand to a smooth finish with a drum sander in your drill.

9 Rout a ¼"-deep rectangular area in the back of the top section face frame to receive the glass panel. Using a hammer and a chisel, square the routed corners.

10 Nail the sides of the top section to the front of the top section. Then, nail the clock panel spacers to the inside of the top section. This creates a 1½" space between the inside clock panel and the glass that will be mounted in the front face frame.

11 Draw lines at the bottom of the face-frame arch on the face-frame stiles, then rout the inside and outside edges of the face frame with a ¼" roundover bit. Be sure to stop at the pencil lines when routing the outside edges as shown in the photo.

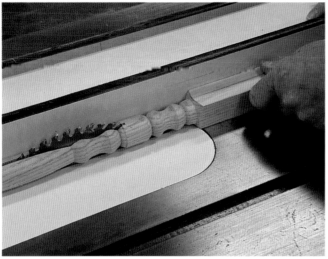

12 Rip a 1⅛" stair spindle in half with your table saw. You can purchase stair spindles at most home-improvement stores.

13 Cut the spindles approximately 11¼"-long.

14 Screw the top mid-section divider to the base of the top section. Then glue and nail the two half spindles to the front of the top section.

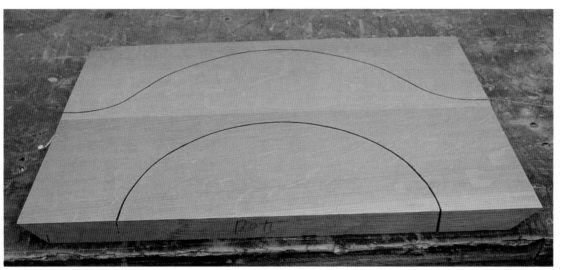

15 Make 45° cuts on the sides of the subcrown moulding blank. Then, make a template for the subcrown moulding per the technical drawing, trace the pattern on the blank, cut out with a jigsaw and sand.

16 Attach the side subcrown moulding. Then, nail the front subcrown moulding onto the side subcrown moulding and the top section.

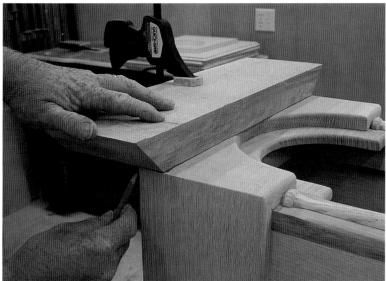

17 Cut the crown moulding on a 45° angle on each side to fit the subcrown moulding. Lay the crown moulding blank on the subcrown moulding, lipping it 1¼" down from the top outside edges of the subcrown moulding. Use a pencil to trace the arc of the subcrown moulding onto the crown moulding.

18 Cut out the arc of the crown moulding, then make a new mark 1¼" down on the face of the crown moulding. Cut out with your jigsaw, and you'll have a 1¼" crown moulding piece. Now use the sanding drum in your drill to sand the inside of the arc.

20 Finish sand the top of the crown and subcrown mouldings to a nice, smooth finish.

19 Glue the crown moulding onto the subcrown moulding face and sides. Do not use nails, as this crown moulding will have a router detail added later.

21 Disassemble the clock you purchased. Trace around the trim ring, and cut a hole in the inside clock panel to accept the clock. Locate the clock in the panel for the best appearance.

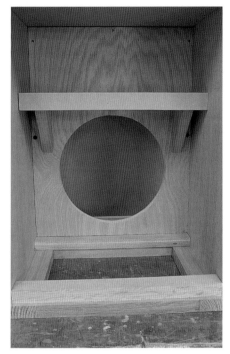

22 Screw the inside clock panel to the clock panel spacers that you installed earlier. Note the secret shelf above the clock. It can be accessed up through the clock's midsection.

23 Screw the finished top section onto the midsection. The clamp is attached to the crown moulding spacer strip (which is is the same thickness as the door). When the crown moulding is attached to this strip, the crown moulding will appear to go around the door instead of the clock body.

24 Use your router and a 1/2" cove router bit to rout the crown moulding. Use two different settings on the router to cut the crown moulding. First, cut the lower cove. This is a deep cut, so you might want to make the cut in two shallower cuts. Be careful to not touch the face frame with the router bit. Then, lower the router base (which "raises" the bit), and make the second cove cut. This cut is much shallower than the first. Using this method is a simple but effective way to make an attractive moulding.

25 Attach the crown moulding to the base of the upper case and the base of the middle case with glue and nails. Build the doors as shown in the "Alternative Woodworking Techniques" pages 9-10. Fill all nails holes, finish sand, stain and finish the clock. Install the glass in the clock face frame and the door. Then, install the clock works. Screw the back onto the top section, hang the doors and you're ready to keep track of time in style.

bathroom storage cabinet

with accent mirror

A great place to pick up some additional storage space is in the bathroom. With its accent mirror and captain's rail detail, this cabinet has room for hand towels, bath towels and other toiletries, plus it has a place for bathroom plants and other colorful decorative favorites. This cabinet is stained a light oak color, but it also could be painted to match any bathroom décor.

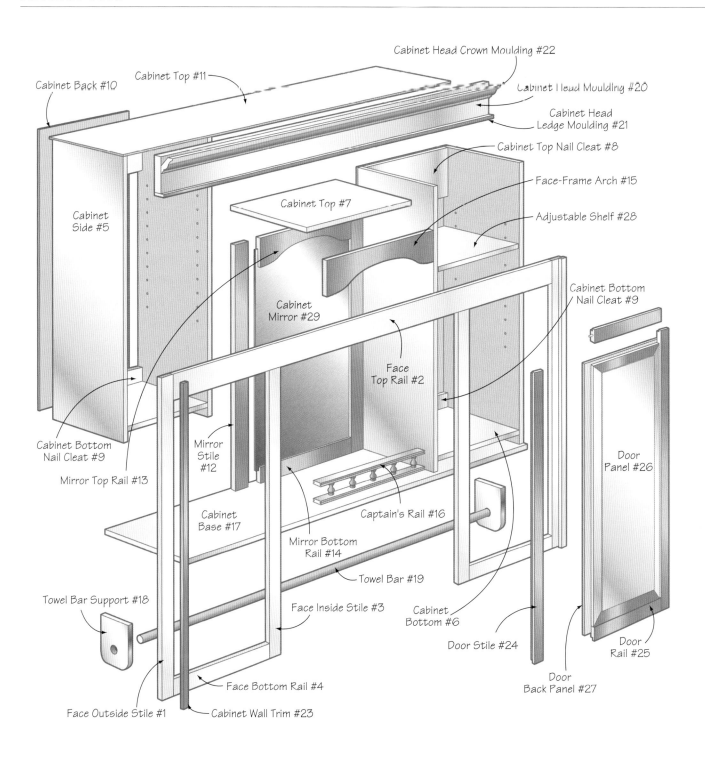

Cabinet Head Crown Moulding #22

Cabinet Back #10   Cabinet Top #11

Cabinet Head Moulding #20

Cabinet Head
Ledge Moulding #21

Cabinet Top Nail Cleat #8

Cabinet
Side #5

Face-Frame Arch #15

Cabinet Top #7

Adjustable Shelf #28

Cabinet Bottom
Nail Cleat #9

Cabinet
Mirror #29

Face
Top Rail #2

Cabinet Bottom
Nail Cleat #9

Mirror
Stile
#12

Mirror Top Rail #13

Door
Panel #26

Cabinet
Base #17

Captain's Rail #16

Mirror Bottom
Rail #14

Towel Bar #19

Towel Bar Support #18

Face Inside Stile #3

Cabinet
Bottom #6

Door Stile #24

Door
Rail #25

Door
Back Panel #27

Face Outside Stile #1   Cabinet Wall Trim #23   Face Bottom Rail #4

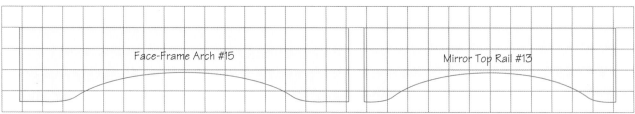

Face-Frame Arch #15   Mirror Top Rail #13

1 square = 1"

cutting list INCHES

REFERENCE	QUANTITY	PART	STOCK	THICKNESS	WIDTH	LENGTH	COMMENTS
1	2	Face Outside Stiles	Oak	$3/4$	$1^1/2$	32	
2	1	Face Top Rail	Oak	$3/4$	$7^1/4$	$37^1/4$	
3	2	Face Inside Stiles	Oak	$3/4$	$1^1/2$	$24^3/4$	
4	2	Face Bottom Rails	Oak	$3/4$	2	9	
5	4	Cabinet Sides	Oak Ply.*	$3/4$	7	32	
6	2	Cabinet Bottoms	Oak Ply.	$3/4$	7	$10^1/4$	
7	1	Cabinet Top	Oak Ply.	$3/4$	7	$16^1/4$	
8	2	Cabinet Top Nail Cleats	Oak Ply.	$3/4$	8	$10^1/4$	
9	2	Cabinet Bottom Nail Cleats	Oak Ply.	$3/4$	$2^1/2$	$10^1/4$	
10	2	Cabinet Backs	Oak Ply.	$1/4$	$11^3/4$	32	
11	1	Cabinet Top	Oak Ply.	$1/4$	8	$39^3/4$	
12	2	Mirror Stiles	Oak	$3/4$	2	$24^3/4$	
13	1	Mirror Top Rail	Oak	$3/4$	$3^1/2$	$12^1/4$	A
14	1	Mirror Bottom Rail	Oak	$3/4$	2	$12^1/4$	
15	1	Face-Frame Arch	Oak	$3/4$	$3^1/2$	$16^1/4$	A
16	1	Captain's Rail	Oak	$3/4$	2	$16^1/4$	B
17	1	Cabinet Base	Oak	$3/4$	9	41	C
18	2	Towel Bar Supports	Oak	$3/4$	4	5	
19	1	Towel Bar	Oak	1" dia.		36	B
20	1	Cabinet Head Moulding	Oak Ply.	$3/4$	5	41	C
21	1	Cabinet Head Ledge Moulding	Oak	$3/8$	$1^1/4$	41	C
22	1	Cabinet Head Crown Moulding	Oak	$1/2$	$1^5/8$	41	B, C
23	2	Cabinet Wall Trim	Oak	$1/4$	$3/4$	$26^7/8$	
24	4	Door Stiles	Oak	$3/4$	2	$25^1/4$	
25	4	Door Rails	Oak	$3/4$	2	$5^1/2$	
26	2	Door Inset Panels	Oak	$3/4$	$5^1/2$	$21^1/4$	
27	2	Door Back Panels	Oak Ply.	$1/4$	$9^1/2$	$25^1/4$	
28	2	Adjustable Shelves	Oak Ply.	$3/4$	$6^7/8$	$10^1/8$	
29	1	Cabinet Mirror	Mirror	$1/8$	$12^7/8$	$21^1/2$	C

*Plywood

A: Cut to pattern design

B: Purchase at local home-improvement store

C: Cut length to fit

HARDWARE:

4 $3/8$" backset hinges

2 door pulls

8 - $1/4$" shelf supports

1 - $1/8$" mirror cut to fit frame

cutting list MILLIMETERS

REFERENCE	QUANTITY	PART	STOCK	THICKNESS	WIDTH	LENGTH	COMMENTS
1	2	Face Outside Stiles	Oak	19	38	813	
2	1	Face Top Rail	Oak	19	184	946	
3	2	Face Inside Stiles	Oak	19	38	629	
4	2	Face Bottom Rails	Oak	19	51	229	
5	4	Cabinet Sides	Oak Ply.*	19	178	813	
6	2	Cabinet Bottoms	Oak Ply.	19	178	260	
7	1	Cabinet Top	Oak Ply.	19	178	419	
8	2	Cabinet Top Nail Cleats	Oak Ply.	19	203	260	
9	2	Cabinet Bottom Nail Cleats	Oak Ply.	19	64	260	
10	2	Cabinet Backs	Oak Ply.	6	298	813	
11	1	Cabinet Top	Oak Ply.	6	203	1010	
12	2	Mirror Stiles	Oak	19	51	629	
13	1	Mirror Top Rail	Oak	19	89	311	A
14	1	Mirror Bottom Rail	Oak	19	51	311	
15	1	Face-Frame Arch	Oak	19	89	419	A
16	1	Captain's Rail	Oak	19	51	419	B
17	1	Cabinet Base	Oak	19	229	1041	C
18	2	Towel Bar Supports	Oak	19	102	127	
19	1	Towel Bar	Oak	25 mm dia.		914	B
20	1	Cabinet Head Moulding	Oak Ply.	19	127	1041	C
21	1	Cabinet Head Ledge Moulding	Oak	10	32	1041	C
22	1	Cabinet Head Crown Moulding	Oak	13	41	1041	B, C
23	2	Cabinet Wall Trim	Oak	6	19	682	
24	4	Door Stiles	Oak	19	51	641	
25	4	Door Rails	Oak	19	51	140	
26	2	Door Inset Panels	Oak	19	140	539	
27	2	Door Back Panels	Oak Ply.	6	242	641	
28	2	Adjustable Shelves	Oak Ply.	19	174	257	
29	1	Cabinet Mirror	Mirror	3	327	546	C

*Plywood

A: Cut to pattern design

B: Purchase at local home-improvement store

C: Cut length to fit

HARDWARE:

4 - 10 mm backset hinges

2 door pulls

8 - 6 mm shelf supports

1- 3 mm mirror cut to fit frame

tip When you measure for a built-in cabinet, always allow ¼" on each side for installation. After installation, you can hide the ¼" gap with the cabinet wall trim.

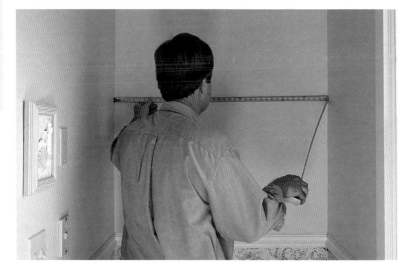

1 Measure the wall space above the bathroom toilet, or wherever it is you will be installing this cabinet. Subtract ½" from this measurement (you want to have the cabinet width ½" less than the opening it will be hung in). Adjust all cabinet measurements accordingly.

2 Cut and assemble the face-frame pieces. See "Alternative Woodworking Methods," pages 9-10, for details.

3 Cut the arch in the mirror top rail per the technical drawing, then sand smooth with your drill and drum sander.

tip Always be aware of doors opening into the room, door trim or anything else that could hinder your access or installation of the cabinet.

4 | Rout a ¼"-deep by ⅜"-wide rabbet into the back of the frame to accept the mirror. Square the corners with a hammer and a chisel.

5 | Round over the inside face of the mirror frame with your router and a ¼" roundover bit.

6 | Make a drilling jig out of scrap wood. Using the jig, space the ¼" holes 2" apart and ⅜"-deep and drill holes for the adjustable shelf supports.

7 | Assemble the body of the cabinet. Then, apply glue to the front edge of the cabinet body and attach the face frame with nails.

8 As you attach the face frame, notice that it overhangs the cabinet body by ¼" on either side. This will give you some additional clearance during installation.

9 Presand the cabinet (with your finish sander) in the location the mirror frame will be placed.

10 Place the cabinet body facedown and nail in the mirror frame.

11 Place the cabinet body faceup. Use a ¼" roundover bit to round over the cabinet face frame edges.

12 Attach the face-frame arch with nails. Inset the arch ¾" from the face of the cabinet.

13 On your workbench, preassemble the three parts of the cabinet head moulding assembly. This assembly will be attached after you've installed the cabinet.

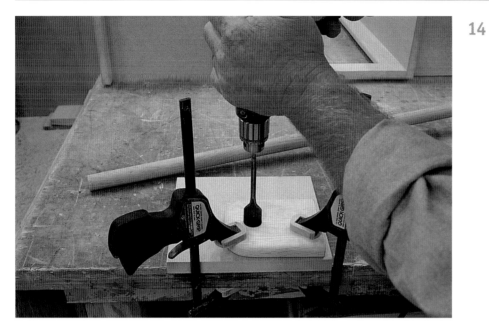

14 Drill the holes for the cabinet towel bar in the towel bar supports using your hand drill and a 1" wood spade bit.

15 Predrill screw holes in the cabinet base for the towel bar supports. Attach the towel bar supports to the base, then install the 1" towel bar dowel. You will attach this finished base assembly after you've installed the cabinet. The towel bar supports should be inset 3" from each side of the cabinet base.

Make the doors (see "Alternative Woodworking Techniques", pages 9-10). Finish sand, stain and apply finish to the all parts.

Note: install the mirror before installing the cabinet.

16 When installing the cabinet, support it on temporary boards cut to the necessary length. Use caution and don't let the cabinet fall before you've screwed it to the wall! Screw though the nail cleats and be sure the screws go into the wall studs at least 1½".

17 Cut the cabinet head moulding assembly ¹⁄₁₆" less than the wall width. Nail this onto the cabinet.

18 Cut the towel bar assembly ¹⁄₁₆" less than the wall width. Screw this onto the cabinet.

19 Cut the cabinet wall trim to fit between the head moulding and the cabinet base. Attach this to the cabinet face frame with finish nails. Hang the doors, install the shelves and you're done.

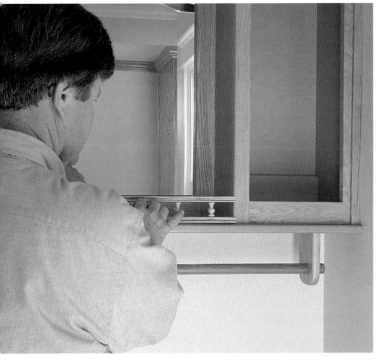

20 After you've cut the captain's rail to length, attach it to the cabinet with small finish nails.

display case

Many of us have things we would like to display, such as ceramic dolls, the kids' trophies or, in Frank and Connie Andermahr's case, antique martini shakers. Unfortunately, projects such as this often turn out to be more of a hutch than a display case. Why not build a display case that will really show off your treasures?

The three arched glass doors and fluted trim give this piece a striking look. The three drawers add additional storage space that makes this project practical as well as pleasing.

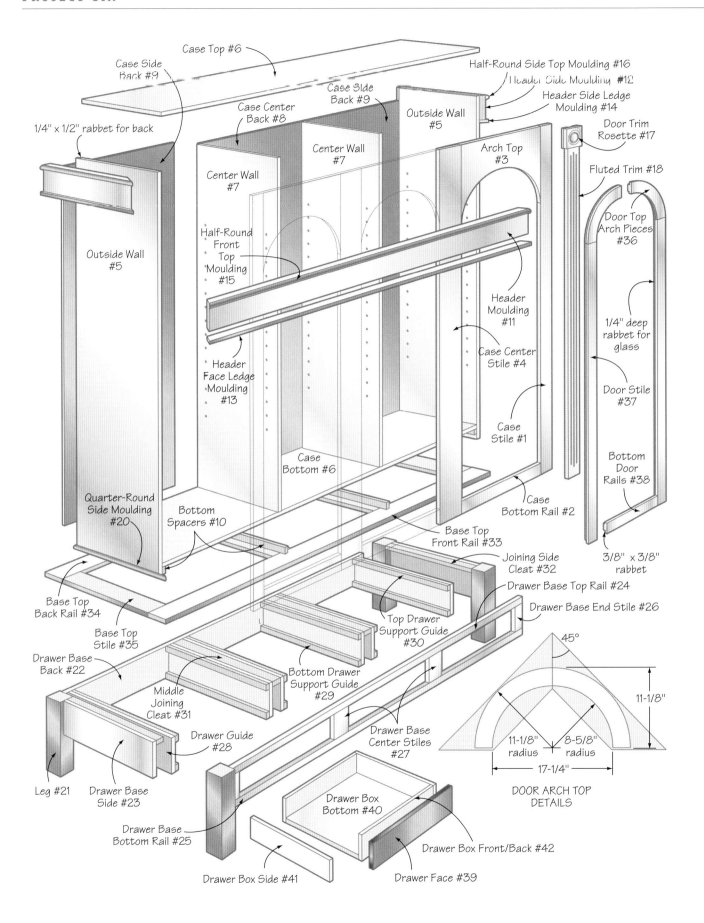

Case Top #6

Case Side Back #9

Half-Round Side Top Moulding #16

Header Side Moulding #12

Header Side Ledge Moulding #14

Case Side Back #9

Case Center Back #8

Outside Wall #5

Door Trim Rosette #17

1/4" x 1/2" rabbet for back

Center Wall #7

Center Wall #7

Arch Top #3

Fluted Trim #18

Door Top Arch Pieces #36

Half-Round Front Top Moulding #15

Outside Wall #5

Header Moulding #11

1/4" deep rabbet for glass

Header Face Ledge Moulding #13

Case Center Stile #4

Door Stile #37

Case Stile #1

Quarter-Round Side Moulding #20

Bottom Spacers #10

Case Bottom #6

Bottom Door Rails #38

Case Bottom Rail #2

3/8" x 3/8" rabbet

Base Top Front Rail #33

Joining Side Cleat #32

Drawer Base Top Rail #24

Base Top Back Rail #34

Top Drawer Support Guide #30

Drawer Base End Stile #26

Base Top Stile #35

45°

Drawer Base Back #22

Middle Joining Cleat #31

Bottom Drawer Support Guide #29

11-1/8"

Drawer Guide #28

Drawer Base Center Stiles #27

11-1/8" radius

8-5/8" radius

Leg #21

Drawer Base Side #23

17-1/4"

DOOR ARCH TOP DETAILS

Drawer Base Bottom Rail #25

Drawer Box Bottom #40

Drawer Box Front/Back #42

Drawer Box Side #41

Drawer Face #39

cutting list INCHES

REFERENCE	QUANTITY	PART	STOCK	THICKNESS	WIDTH	LENGTH	COMMENTS
1	2	Case Stiles	Alder	3/4	4	71	
2	3	Case Bottom Rails	Alder	3/4	2	21³/4	
3	3	Case Arch Tops	Alder	3/4	17	21³/4	Cut to design
4	2	Case Center Stiles	Alder	3/4	5¹/4	71	
5	2	Case Outsides	Alder Ply.*	3/4	15	71	¹/4" x ¹/2" dado on inside back edges of sides
6	2	Case Top & Bottom	Alder Ply.	3/4	14³/4	82¹/4	
7	2	Case Center Walls	Alder Ply.	3/4	14³/4	65¹/2	
8	1	Case Center Back	Alder Ply.	¹/4	27	68¹/4	
9	2	Case Side Backs	Alder Ply.	¹/4	28	68¹/4	
10	4	Bottom Spacers	Any	3/4	1¹/4	14³/4	
11	1	Header Face Moulding	Alder	3/4	4¹/2	88	Cut to fit on 45°
12	2	Header Side Moulding	Alder	3/4	4¹/2	19	Cut to fit on 45°
13	1	Header Face Ledge Moulding	Alder	3/8	1¹/4	88	Cut to fit on 45°
14	2	Header Side Ledge Moulding	Alder	3/8	1¹/4	19	Cut to fit on 45°
15	1	Half-Round Face Top Moulding	Alder	3/4	1	88	Cut to fit on 45°
16	2	Half-Round Side Top Moulding	Alder	3/4	1	19	Cut to fit on 45°
17	4	Door Trim Rosettes	Alder	7/8	2³/4	2³/4	Purchase at local home-improvement store
18	4	Fluted Trim	Alder	3/4	2³/4	63³/4	
19	1	Quarter-Round Front Moulding	Alder	¹/2	¹/2	96	Cut pieces to fit around the fluted columns
20	2	Quarter-Round Side Moulding	Alder	¹/2	¹/2	24	Cut to fit on 45°
21	4	Legs	Alder	3¹/4	3¹/4	13¹/4	
22	1	Drawer Base Back	Alder	3/4	7³/4	78¹/2	
23	2	Drawer Base Sides	Alder	3/4	7³/4	10³/4	
24	1	Drawer Base Top Rail	Alder	3/4	2	78¹/2	
25	1	Drawer Base Bottom Rail	Alder	3/4	1³/4	78¹/2	
26	2	Drawer Base End Stiles	Alder	3/4	1¹/4	4	
27	2	Drawer Base Center Stiles	Alder	3/4	5¹/4	4	
28	6	Drawer Guides	Any Ply.	3/4	7³/4	14³/4	
29	6	Drawer Bottom Support Guides	Any Ply.	3/4	1³/4	14³/4	
30	6	Drawer Top Support Guides	Any Ply.	3/4	2	14³/4	
31	2	Middle Joining Cleats	Any Ply.	3/4	3³/4	14³/4	
32	2	Side Joining Cleats	Any Ply.	3/4	1³/4	10³/4	
33	1	Base Top Front Rail	Alder	3/4	4	86¹/2	
34	1	Base Top Back Rail	Alder	3/4	3	86¹/2	
35	4	Base Top Stiles	Alder	3/4	4	11¹/8	
36	6	Door Top Arch Pieces	Alder	3/4	5¹/2	23	Cut to design; cut to fit on 45°
37	6	Door Stiles	Alder	3/4	2¹/2	52¹/2	
38	3	Bottom Door Rails	Alder	3/4	2¹/2	17¹/4	
39	3	Drawer Faces	Alder	3/4	4¹/2	22³/8	
40	3	Drawer Box Bottoms	Melamine	3/4	13	20³/4	
41	6	Drawer Box Sides	Melamine	¹/2	3⁷/8	14	
42	6	Drawer Box Fronts & Backs	Melamine	¹/2	3⁷/8	20³/4	

*Plywood

HARDWARE:

25' of 5/8"-wide edge banding to match the color of melamine PB

9 - 3/8" backset hinges

36 - ¹/4" shelf supports

3 door pulls

3 - ¹/8" tempered glass arch panels (cut to fit)

3 drawer pulls

9 - ¹/4" tempered glass shelves (cut to fit)

cutting list MILLIMETERS

REFERENCE	QUANTITY	PART	STOCK	THICKNESS	WIDTH	LENGTH	COMMENTS
1	2	Case Stiles	Alder	19	102	1803	
2	3	Case Bottom Rails	Alder	19	51	552	
3	3	Case Arch Tops	Alder	19	432	552	Cut to design
4	2	Case Center Stiles	Alder	19	133	1803	
5	2	Case Outsides	Alder Ply.*	19	381	1803	6 x 13mm dado on inside back edges of sides
6	2	Case Top & Bottom	Alder Ply.	19	362	2089	
7	2	Case Center Walls	Alder Ply.	19	362	1664	
8	1	Case Center Back	Alder Ply.	6	686	1733	
9	2	Case Side Backs)	Alder Ply.	6	711	1733	
10	4	Bottom Spacers	Any	19	32	375	
11	1	Header Face Moulding	Alder	19	115	2235	Cut to fit on 45°
12	2	Header Side Moulding	Alder	19	115	483	Cut to fit on 45°
13	1	Header Face Ledge Moulding	Alder	10	32	2235	Cut to fit on 45°
14	2	Header Side Ledge Moulding	Alder	10	32	483	Cut to fit on 45°
15	1	Half-Round Face Top Moulding	Alder	19	25	2235	Cut to fit on 45°
16	2	Half-Round Side Top Moulding	Alder	19	25	483	Cut to fit on 45°
17	4	Door Trim Rosettes	Alder	22	70	70	Purchase at local home-improvement store
18	4	Fluted Trim	Alder	19	70	1619	
19	1	Quarter-Round Moulding	Alder	13	6	2438	Cut pieces to fit around the fluted columns
20	2	Quarter-Round Moulding	Alder	13	6	610	Cut to fit on 45°
21	4	Legs	Alder	82	82	336	
22	1	Drawer Base Back	Alder	19	197	1994	
23	2	Drawer Base Sides	Alder	19	197	273	
24	1	Drawer Base Top Rail	Alder	19	51	1994	
25	1	Drawer Base Bottom Rail	Alder	19	45	1994	
26	2	Drawer Base End Stiles	Alder	19	32	102	
27	2	Drawer Base Center Stiles	Alder	19	133	102	
28	6	Drawer Guides	Any Ply.	19	197	375	
29	6	Drawer Bottom Support Guides	Any Ply.	19	45	375	
30	6	Drawer Top Support Guides	Any Ply.	19	51	375	
31	2	Middle Joining Cleats	Any Ply.	19	82	375	
32	2	Side Joining Cleats	Any Ply.	19	45	273	
33	1	Base Top Front Rail	Alder	19	102	2197	
34	1	Base Top Back Rail	Alder	19	76	3197	
35	4	Base Top Stiles	Alder	19	102	295	
36	6	Door Top Arch Pieces	Alder	19	140	584	Cut to design; cut to fit on 45°
37	6	Door Stiles	Alder	19	64	1333	
38	3	Bottom Door Rails	Alder	19	64	438	
39	3	Drawer Faces	Alder	19	115	575	
40	3	Drawer Box Bottom	Melamine	19	330	527	
41	6	Drawer Box Sides	Melamine	13	98	356	
42	6	Drawer Box Fronts & Backs	Melamine	13	98	527	

*Plywood

HARDWARE:

7.5m of 16mm-wide edge banding to match the color of melamine PB

9 - 10mm backset hinges

36 - 6mm shelf supports

3 door pulls

3 - 3mm tempered glass arch panels (cut to fit)

3 drawer pulls

9 - 6mm tempered glass shelves (cut to fit)

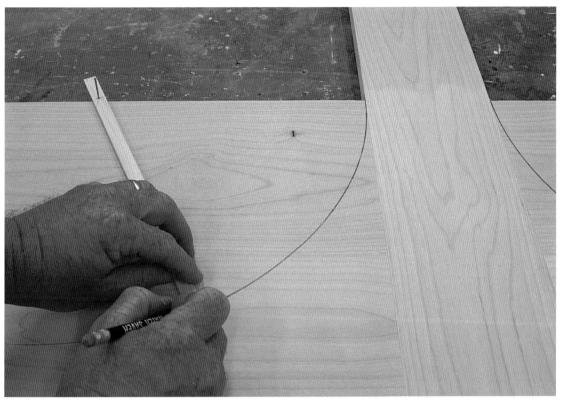

1 | Assemble the face frame, then use a scrap piece of wood for a compass and trace the arch on the face frame to be cut out. Note that the radius of the arch is one-half the length of the arch top piece.

2 | After cutting out the arch, sand the inside of it smooth with your drill and sanding drum.

tip This project is a very large piece of furniture. Before you begin, be sure that it will fit through your doors after it is completed. The drawer base can be removed for handling, which will shorten it by $13\frac{1}{4}''$.

3 | Make a pattern out of scrap wood and drill ¼" holes 2" apart and ⅜"-deep. Then use the pattern to drill the holes for the adjustable shelf brackets in the case outsides and the case center walls.

4 | Assemble the cabinet body and attach the face frame. Then, assemble the front and side header moulding pieces (the half-round top moulding, header moulding and the header moulding face ledge). Then cut these head moulding assemblies at 45° angles at the corners and attach with nails. Make sure that the top edge of the header is flush with the case top.

5 | Make your router setup using a ⅜" fluting bit in your router and a scrap piece of wood 2¾" wide. When you have the spacing and depth correct, rout the flutes in your four fluted trim pieces. (If you don't have a router table, just mount your router to a ½" piece of particleboard with four legs to support the table. This will work just as well.)

6 As you rout the flutes into the fluted trim, it is almost impossible to avoid router burns. A great way to sand out those burns is to use a Dremel #114 bit in your drill.

7 Use door-trim rosettes at the top of the fluted trim. These can be purchased at any local home-improvement store. To create an offset look, you may need to add ¼" to the rosettes to build them up to 1" thick. This will create a nice stepped look on the front of the cabinet.

8 Using the pocket-hole drill guide, drill holes on the drawer base front, back and sides, then screw the pieces to the four legs. The drawer base front, back and sides are set in from the outside edges of the legs ¾".

9 Attach the drawer supports to the drawer guides, then nail the assembly into the drawer base.

10 Glue and nail the joining cleats flush with the top of the drawer base. Now, assemble the base top frame and rout a ¼" roundover on the top and bottom edges of the sides and front of the frame. Then, attach the frame to the bottom of the upper case with glue and nails.

11 Use ½" quarter-rounds to trim the bottoms of the fluted trim. This helps blend the fluted trim into the base of the cabinet.

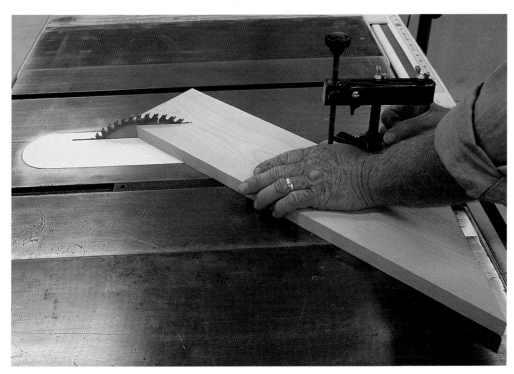

12 | Using the miter jig on your table saw, cut the door top arch pieces 23" long at the outside of the 45° miters.

13 | Use a scrap piece of plywood to hold the door top arch pieces at a right angle. Draw a line straight across the plywood at the bottom of the arch door tops. Nail a scrap piece of wood for a compass to the center of that line with the nail $8\frac{5}{8}$" from the end of the compass. Trace the arch as shown. Then set the nail at $11\frac{1}{8}$" and trace the second arch.

14 | Cut $\frac{3}{4}$" notches into the door top arch pieces to allow for clamping, then dowel and glue the top arch pieces together. Make sure the dowels stay inside the lines. Clamp as shown.

15 Dowel and glue the bottom door rail to the door stiles, then dowel and glue the door top arch pieces to the side stiles. Clamp as shown.

16 Cut the door top arches with your jigsaw.

17 Sand the outer edges of the arch doors with your belt sander.

tip When you clamp the arch door assemblies together, be extra careful that the door pieces glue together flat.

18 Sand the inner edge of the arch doors with your drill and drum sander.

19 Round over the inside and outside edges of the door face with your router and a ¼" roundover bit.

20 Use your router and a ⅜" rabbeting bit to rout a ⅜"-deep by ⅜"-wide rabbet on the outside edges of the back of the door for the ⅜" backset hinge. Test fit the door and make any adjustments, i.e., you may need to make the outside rabbet a little deeper if this routed part doesn't fit into the cabinet opening. (The door should lip over the cabinet opening.) Then rout a ¼"-deep by ⅜"-wide rabbet on the inside back of the door to accept the glass. Square the inside routed corners with a hammer and a chisel.

21 Assemble the drawers using glue and nails. Rout a ¼" roundover on the outside edges of the drawer front. Then, attach the drawer fronts with screws from the inside of the drawer box front.

I used a dark cherry stain on this cabinet and then applied the finish.

The upper case just sits on top of the base and is heavy enough to stay in place. However, if you like, insert four 2½" screws up through the drawer base top rail into the base top rail. Install the glass in the doors and hang the doors. Finally, install the drawers and your done.

One last feature that you might choose to add to this cabinet is flush-mounting lights in the top of the three upper sections of the cabinet. These lights will shine down through the glass shelves and create a wonderful effect.

dresser
with television cabinet

Most of today's bedrooms either have room for a large dresser or room for a television cabinet — but not both. With this unique project, you get the best of both worlds.

This is a surprisingly easy piece to build because of its three-piece sectional design. It has six large dresser drawers in the base cabinet, and the upper left linen portion has a place for a VCR or DVD unit, as well as room for sweaters and bedspreads.

The upper right portion easily conceals a 19" television behind tambour doors. You'll really appreciate the storage and the organization that exists in this piece of furniture.

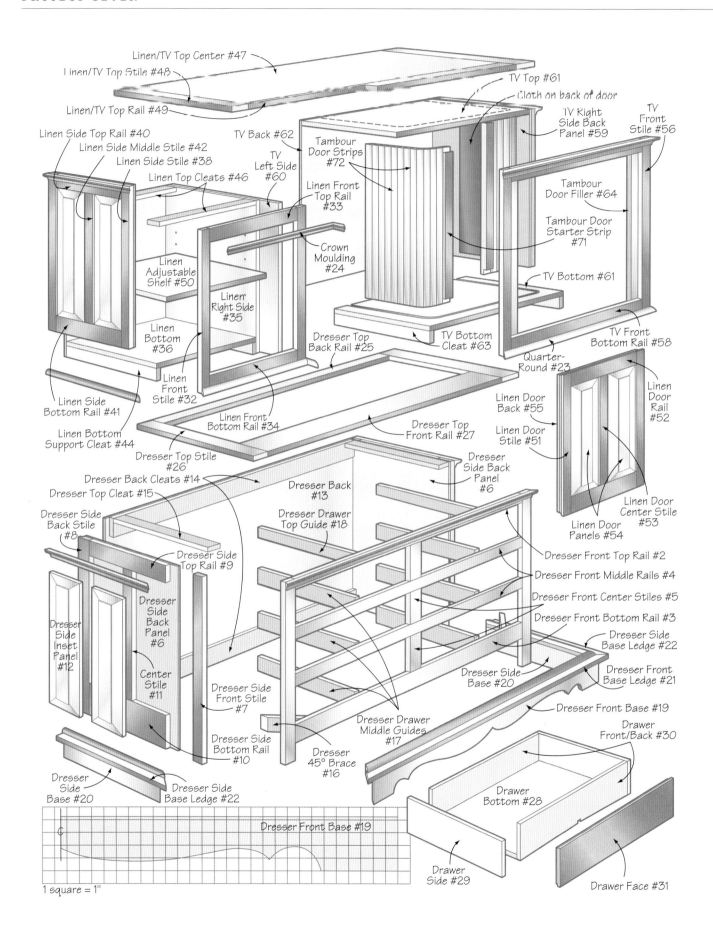

Linen/TV Top Center #47

Linen/TV Top Stile #48

Linen/TV Top Rail #49

TV Top #61

Cloth on back of door

Linen Side Top Rail #40

Linen Side Middle Stile #42

Linen Side Stile #38

Linen Top Cleats #46

TV Back #62

TV Left Side #60

Tambour Door Strips #72

TV Right Side Back Panel #59

TV Front Stile #56

Linen Front Top Rail #33

Tambour Door Filler #64

Tambour Door Starter Strip #71

Linen Adjustable Shelf #50

Crown Moulding #24

Linen Right Side #35

TV Bottom #61

Linen Bottom #36

Dresser Top Back Rail #25

TV Bottom Cleat #63

TV Front Bottom Rail #58

Linen Front Stile #32

Quarter-Round #23

Linen Door Back #55

Linen Door Rail #52

Linen Side Bottom Rail #41

Linen Front Bottom Rail #34

Dresser Top Front Rail #27

Linen Door Stile #51

Linen Bottom Support Cleat #44

Dresser Top Stile #26

Dresser Back Cleats #14

Dresser Top Cleat #15

Dresser Back #13

Dresser Side Back Panel #6

Linen Door Center Stile #53

Linen Door Panels #54

Dresser Side Back Stile #8

Dresser Drawer Top Guide #18

Dresser Front Top Rail #2

Dresser Side Top Rail #9

Dresser Front Middle Rails #4

Dresser Front Center Stiles #5

Dresser Side Inset Panel #12

Dresser Side Back Panel #6

Dresser Front Bottom Rail #3

Dresser Side Base Ledge #22

Center Stile #11

Dresser Side Front Stile #7

Dresser Side Base #20

Dresser Front Base Ledge #21

Dresser Front Base #19

Drawer Front/Back #30

Dresser Side Bottom Rail #10

Dresser Drawer Middle Guides #17

Dresser 45° Brace #16

Dresser Side Base #20

Dresser Side Base Ledge #22

Dresser Front Base #19

Drawer Bottom #28

Drawer Side #29

Drawer Face #31

1 square = 1"

cutting list INCHES

REFERENCE	QUANTITY	PART	STOCK	THICKNESS	WIDTH	LENGTH	COMMENTS
1	2	Dresser Front Stiles	Oak	3/4	1 1/2	32	
2	1	Dresser Front Top Rail	Oak	3/4	2 3/4	49	
3	1	Dresser Front Bottom Rail	Oak	3/4	3 1/2	49	
4	2	Dresser Front Middle Rails	Oak	3/4	2	49	
5	3	Dresser Front Center Stiles	Oak	3/4	2	6	
6	2	Dresser Side Back Panels	Plywood	1/4	20 1/4	32	
7	2	Dresser Side Front Stiles	Oak	3/4	1 1/4	32	
8	2	Dresser Side Back Stiles	Oak	3/4	2	32	
9	2	Dresser Side Top Rails	Oak	3/4	2 3/4	17	
10	2	Dresser Side Bottom Rails	Oak	3/4	7	17	
11	2	Dresser Side Middle Stiles	Oak	3/4	2	22 1/4	
12	4	Dresser Side Inset Panels	Oak	3/4	7 1/2	22 1/4	
13	1	Dresser Back	Plywood	1/4	32	51 1/4	
14	2	Dresser Back Cleats	Poplar	3/4	3 1/2	50	
15	2	Dresser Top Cleats	Poplar	3/4	2	19 1/4	
16	2	Dresser 45° Braces	Poplar	3/4	2	8	
17	6	Dresser Drawer Middle Guides	Poplar	3/4	2 3/8	20	
18	2	Dresser Drawer Top Guides	Poplar	3/4	2 3/4	19 1/4	
19	1	Dresser Front Base	Oak	3/4	4 1/4	55	A
20	2	Dresser Side Bases	Oak	3/4	4 1/4	23	B
21	1	Dresser Front Base Ledge	Oak	3/4	1 1/4	55	
22	2	Dresser Side Base Ledges	Oak	3/4	1 1/4	23	
23	2	Quarter-Round Moulding Trim	Oak	1/2	1/2	108	B
24	2	Crown Moulding Trim	Oak	1/2	1 5/8	108	C
25	1	Dresser Top Back Rail	Poplar	3/4	2 1/2	48 1/4	
26	2	Dresser Top Stiles	Oak	3/4	3 1/4	22 1/2	
27	1	Dresser Top Front Rail	Oak	3/4	6	48 1/4	
28	6	Drawer Bottoms	Melamine	3/4	20 1/4	22	
29	12	Drawer Sides	Melamine	1/2	5 7/8	20 1/4	
30	12	Drawer Fronts & Backs	Melamine	1/2	5 1/8	22	
31	6	Drawer Faces	Oak	3/4	6 1/2	24	
32	2	Linen Front Stiles	Oak	3/4	1 1/2	23 3/4	
33	1	Linen Front Top Rail	Oak	3/4	2 3/4	18	
34	1	Linen Front Bottom Rail	Oak	3/4	2	18	
35	1	Linen Right Side	Oak Ply.	3/4	17	23 3/4	
36	1	Linen Bottom	Oak Ply.	3/4	17	19 1/4	
37	1	Linen Left Side Back Panel	Oak Ply.	1/4	17 1/4	23 3/4	
38	1	Linen Side Front Stile	Oak	3/4	1 1/4	23 3/4	
39	1	Linen Side Back Stile	Oak	3/4	2	23 3/4	
40	1	Linen Side Top Rail	Oak	3/4	2 3/4	14	
41	1	Linen Side Bottom Rail	Oak	3/4	2	14	
42	1	Linen Side Middle Stile	Oak	3/4	2	19	
43	2	Linen Side Inset Panels	Oak	3/4	6	19	
44	2	Linen Bottom Support Cleats	Poplar	3/4	1 1/4	17	
45	1	Linen Back	Oak Ply.	1/4	20 1/2	23 3/4	
46	2	Linen Top Cleats	Poplar	3/4	2	19 1/4	
47	1	Linen/TV Top Center	Oak Ply.	3/4	17 1/2	46 1/2	
48	2	Linen/TV Top Stiles	Oak	3/4	3 1/4	21 1/2	
49	1	Linen/TV Top Rail	Oak	3/4	4	46 1/2	
50	1	Linen Adjustable Shelf	Oak Ply.	3/4	16 7/8	19 1/8	
51	2	Linen Door Stiles	Oak	3/4	2	19 1/2	
52	2	Linen Door Top & Bottom Rails	Oak	3/4	2	14 1/2	
53	1	Linen Door Center Stile	Oak	3/4	2	15 1/2	
54	2	Linen Door Inset Panels	Oak	3/4	6 1/4	15 1/2	
55	1	Linen Door Back	Oak Ply.	1/4	18 1/2	19 1/2	
56	2	TV Front Stiles	Oak	3/4	1 1/2	23 3/4	
57	1	TV Front Top Rail	Oak	3/4	2 3/4	26	
58	1	TV Front Bottom Rail	Oak	3/4	2	26	
59	1	TV Right Side Back Panel	Oak Ply.	1/4	19	23 3/4	
60	1	TV Left Side	Oak Ply.	3/4	19	23 3/4	
61	2	TV Top & Bottom/ Tambour Door Tracks	Oak Ply.	3/4	19	27 1/4	
62	1	TV Back	Oak Ply.	1/4	23 3/4	28 1/2	
63	2	TV Bottom Cleats	Poplar	3/4	1 1/4	19	
64	2	Tambour Door Fillers	Oak	3/4	1 3/4	21	
65	1	TV Side Front Stile	Oak	3/4	1 1/4	23 3/4	
66	1	TV Side Back Stile	Oak	3/4	2	23 3/4	
67	1	TV Side Top Rail	Oak	3/4	2 3/4	16	
68	1	TV Side Bottom Rail	Oak	3/4	2	16	
69	1	TV Side Middle Stile	Oak	3/4	2	19	
70	2	TV Side Inset Panels	Oak	3/4	7	19	
71	2	Tambour Door Starter Strips	Oak	1/2	1	24	D
72	32	Tambour Door Strips	Oak	1/4	3/4	24	D

*Plywood

A: Cut to length on 45°; cut to design

B: Cut to length on 45°

C: Purchase at local home-improvement store; cut to length on 45°

D: Cut to length after gluing on the canvas

HARDWARE:

50' of 5/8"-wide edge banding to match color of melamine

1- 30" x 36" tambour door canvas; purchase at local material/cloth store

4 - 1/4" shelf support clips

2 - 3/8" backset hinges

3 door knobs

6 drawer pulls

cutting list MILLIMETERS

REFERENCE	QUANTITY	PART	STOCK	THICKNESS	WIDTH	LENGTH	COMMENTS
1	2	Dresser Front Stiles	Oak	19	38	813	
2	1	Dresser Front Top Rail	Oak	19	70	1245	
3	1	Dresser Front Bottom Rail	Oak	19	89	1245	
4	2	Dresser Front Middle Rails	Oak	19	51	1245	
5	3	Dresser Front Center Stiles	Oak	19	51	152	
6	2	Dresser Side Back Panels	Plywood	6	514	813	
7	2	Dresser Side Front Stiles	Oak	19	32	813	
8	2	Dresser Side Back Stiles	Oak	19	51	813	
9	2	Dresser Side Top Rails	Oak	19	70	432	
10	2	Dresser Side Bottom Rails	Oak	19	178	432	
11	2	Dresser Side Middle Stiles	Oak	19	51	565	
12	4	Dresser Side Inset Panels	Oak	19	191	565	
13	1	Dresser Back	Plywood	6	813	1301	
14	2	Dresser Back Cleats	Poplar	19	89	1270	
15	2	Dresser Top Cleats	Poplar	19	51	489	
16	2	Dresser 45° Braces	Poplar	19	51	203	
17	6	Dresser Drawer Middle Guides	Poplar	19	61	508	
18	2	Dresser Drawer Top Guides	Poplar	19	70	489	
19	1	Dresser Front Base	Oak	19	108	1397	A
20	2	Dresser Side Bases	Oak	19	108	584	B
21	1	Dresser Front Base Ledge	Oak	19	32	1397	
22	2	Dresser Side Base Ledges	Oak	19	32	584	
23	2	Quarter-Round Moulding Trim	Oak	13	13	2743	B
24	2	Crown Moulding Trim	Oak	13	41	2743	C
25	1	Dresser Top Back Rail	Poplar	19	64	1225	
26	2	Dresser Top Stiles	Oak	19	82	572	
27	1	Dresser Top Front Rail	Oak	19	152	1225	
28	6	Drawer Bottoms	Melamine	19	514	559	
29	12	Drawer Sides	Melamine	13	149	514	
30	12	Drawer Fronts & Backs	Melamine	13	130	559	
31	6	Drawer Faces	Oak	19	165	610	
32	2	Linen Front Stiles	Oak	19	38	603	
33	1	Linen Front Top Rail	Oak	19	70	457	
34	1	Linen Front Bottom Rail	Oak	19	51	457	
35	1	Linen Right Side	Oak Ply.	19	432	603	
36	1	Linen Bottom	Oak Ply.	19	432	489	
37	1	Linen Left Side Back Panel	Oak Ply.	6	438	603	
38	1	Linen Side Front Stile	Oak	19	32	603	
39	1	Linen Side Back Stile	Oak	19	51	603	
40	1	Linen Side Top Rail	Oak	19	70	356	
41	1	Linen Side Bottom Rail	Oak	19	51	356	
42	1	Linen Side Middle Stile	Oak	19	51	483	
43	2	Linen Side Inset Panels	Oak	19	152	483	
44	2	Linen Bottom Support Cleats	Poplar	19	32	432	
45	1	Linen Back	Oak Ply.	6	521	578	
46	2	Linen Top Cleats	Poplar	19	51	489	

REFERENCE	QUANTITY	PART	STOCK	THICKNESS	WIDTH	LENGTH	COMMENTS
47	1	Linen/TV Top Center	Oak Ply.	19	445	1181	
48	2	Linen/TV Top Stiles	Oak	19	82	546	
49	1	Linen/TV Top Rail	Oak	19	102	1181	
50	1	Linen Adjustable Shelf	Oak Ply.	19	428	486	
51	2	Linen Door Stiles	Oak	19	51	486	
52	2	Linen Door Top & Bottom Rails	Oak	19	51	369	
53	1	Linen Door Center Stile	Oak	19	51	394	
54	2	Linen Door Inset Panels	Oak	19	158	394	
55	1	Linen Door Back	Oak Ply.	6	470	486	
56	2	TV Front Stiles	Oak	19	38	603	
57	1	TV Front Top Rail	Oak	19	70	660	
58	1	TV Front Bottom Rail	Oak	19	158	660	
59	1	TV Right Side Back Panel	Oak Ply.	6	483	603	
60	1	TV Left Side	Oak Ply.	19	483	603	
61	2	TV Top & Bottom/ Tambour Door Tracks	Oak Ply.	19	483	692	
62	1	TV Back	Oak Ply.	6	603	724	
63	2	TV Bottom Cleats	Poplar	19	32	483	
64	2	Tambour Door Fillers	Oak	19	45	533	
65	1	TV Side Front Stile	Oak	19	32	603	
66	1	TV Side Back Stile	Oak	19	51	603	
67	1	TV Side Top Rail	Oak	19	70	406	
68	1	TV Side Bottom Rail	Oak	19	51	406	
69	1	TV Side Middle Stile	Oak	19	51	483	
70	2	TV Side Inset Panels	Oak	19	178	483	
71	2	Tambour Door Starter Strips	Oak	13	25	610	D
72	32	Tambour Door Strips	Oak	6	19	610	D

*Plywood

A: Cut to length on 45°; cut to design

B: Cut to length on 45°

C: Purchase at local home-improvement store; cut to length on 45°

D: Cut to length after gluing on the canvas

HARDWARE:

15m of 16mm-wide edge banding to match color of melamine

1 - 762 x 914 mm tambour door canvas; purchase at local material/cloth store

4 - 6 mm shelf support clips

2 - 10 mm backset hinges

3 door knobs

6 drawer pulls

1 | See "Alternative Woodworking Methods" on pages 9-10 for side panel construction. On the table saw, cut a ¼" notch into the inside back of the the two outside end panels so they can accept the ¼" back panel.

2 | Assemble the face frame of the base cabinet. Then lay the face frame onto the ¼" dresser back panel and trace the face frame onto the back panel. This will give you reference lines for installing the drawer guides.

3 | Glue and nail the face frame to the side panels. Install the back cleats with glue and nails. Then attach the ¼" back panel with the nails. Next, install the top cleats.

4 | Lay out the pattern on the front base and cut it out. Then, install the side and front bases. Cut the front and side base ledges to fit. Glue and attach with nails.

5 | Cut the front and side base quarter-round moulding to fit. Glue and nail.

6 | Assemble the drawers with glue and nails. Then, cut the drawer guide groove in the center of all six drawer bottoms.

7 | Install the drawer guides using an assembled drawer to center the drawer guides. Align the guides horizontally with the lines on the 1/4" back panel.

8 | Using glue and nails, install two 8"-long angle braces in the front lower left and right corners of the base cabinet as shown.

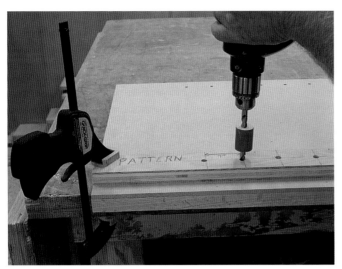

9 Make a drilling jig from a scrap piece of wood with ¼" holes 2" apart for the adjustable shelf brackets. Using this jig, drill ⅜"-deep holes (for the adjustable shelf support clips) in both sides of the linen cabinet section.

10 Assemble the linen cabinet face frame (see "Alternative Woodworking Techniques" on pages 9-10). Assemble the linen cabinet, attach the face frame and install the back.

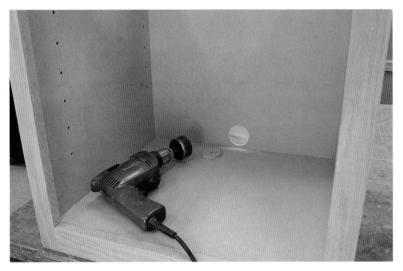

11 With your drill and a 2" hole saw, cut a hole in the lower center back of the linen cabinet back (for the electronic component's wires).

12 To cut the track for the tambour doors, use a scrap piece of plywood for a template. The track is cut ⅜"-deep and ⅜" in from the sides and front edges of the TV's top and bottom panels. Install a ⅜" straight cutting router bit in your router and measure the distance from the edge of your router base to the edge of the bit. Add ¾" to this distance and cut the plywood template to fit this distance in from both of the side edges and the front edge of the TV cabinet's top and bottom panels. Clamp the template to the panel and use it as your guide for the router. Carefully guide the router around the corner of the template to create the curves in the track. The track is a flattened "U" shape (see the technical illustration).

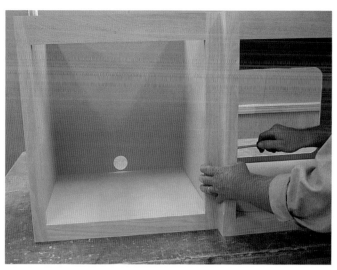

13 Rout a ¼" roundover on the outside front edges of the TV cabinet and the left edge of the linen cabinet. (Use a pipe clamp for a router stop.) Be sure the router bit does not hit the pipe clamp.

14 Screw the linen and TV cabinets together with 1½" screws.

15 Build the dresser top assembly (see "Alternative Woodworking Techniques" page 11). Roundover the top and bottom of both side edges and the front edge using a ¼" roundover bit. Then, attach the assembly to the bottom of the linen/TV cabinet with 1½" screws .

16 Build the top assembly (see "Alternative Woodworking Techniques" page 11). Then, place the cabinet top onto the assembled linen/TV cabinet. Center the top side-to-side and locate the back edge of the top flush to the back of the cabinet assembly. Trace the offset of the linen/TV cabinet onto the bottom of the cabinet top. (Leave the same overhang all around the sides and front of the top.) Cut out the offset with your jigsaw. Sand this cut smooth and roundover the top and bottom of the sides and front edges using a ¼" roundover bit in your router. Screw the top to the linen and TV cabinet assembly.

17 Set your table saw blade to 45°. Set your miter gauge to 90° to cut the crown moulding. When you cut crown moulding on your table saw, pretend that the saw top is the cabinet face and the miter gauge is the cabinet top, then, position the crown moulding to fit that visualized cabinet. Make some test cuts and check the fit.

18 Attach the crown moulding with glue and finish nails.

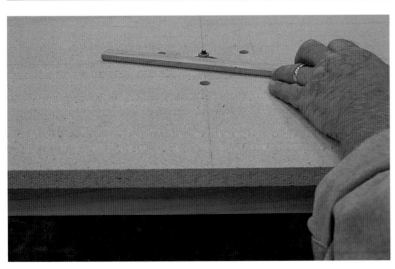

19 Cut the 2 tambour starter strips and all 32 tambour door strips. Round over the two front edges of all 34 strips with a ⅛" roundover bit. Leave the two back edges square. If you don't have a router table, mount your router to a ½" piece of particleboard with four legs to support the table. This works well as a temporary router table.

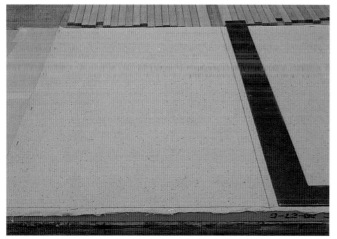

20 Cut a 32" × 38" piece of ½" particleboard. Cover the top of it with wax paper to keep the canvas from sticking to the particleboard when you glue on the tambour strips. Stretch the canvas tightly on the board and tack down the edges. Draw a line on the canvas ¾" in from the edge, parallel with the longer edge of the canvas. Use a square with one edge aligned with the line you just drew, and draw two lines ½" apart to separate the canvas into two equal sides, leaving a ½" space in the center.

21 Begin at the line in the center of the canvas and glue on the tambour door starter strip. Then glue on 16 tambour door strips as shown. Be careful to glue the pieces on the canvas only and not to each other! Repeat this process for the other door, leaving the ½" space in the center. Use weights to hold down the strips while the glue dries.

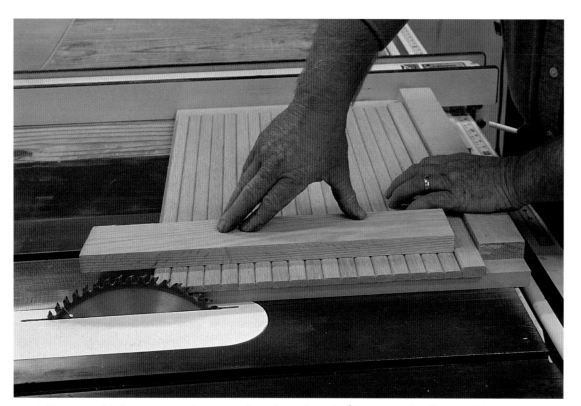

22 Use a razor blade to separate the two tambour doors along the ½" center strip of canvas. To cut one end of the doors square, place the starter strip against the stop of the sliding table jig (see photo #4, page 11), and hold a scrap piece of wood down on top of the tambour door to keep it from vibrating as you trim one edge. Repeat this for the other door.

23 Measure the height inside the TV cabinet and add ⅝" to this measurement. Cut the tambour doors to this height. Hold down the door with a scrap piece of wood as you cut.

24 Trim off ½" of canvas from the top and bottom of each door with a razor blade. Trim off any excess fibers from the back of the starter strip.

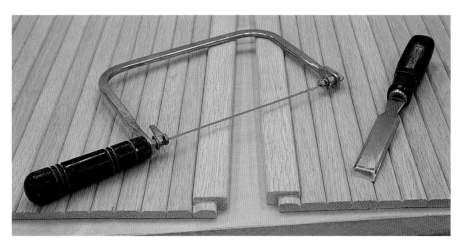

25 Use a coping saw and a chisel to trim ⁷/₁₆" off each end of the starter strips. Cut the end of the starter strip to ¼" × ¾".

26 Slide the tambour doors into the track from the back of the cabinet. Test fit the tambour door fillers. (The tambour door starter strips should just clear the fillers.) Then, attach the tambour door fillers to the back of the face frame to trim the tambour door opening.

Disassemble and sand all the parts. Apply a clear finish. Put the top cabinet onto the dresser. Attach the drawer fronts with screws from the inside of the drawer boxes. Hang the linen cabinet door, install the tambour doors and attach the back to the TV cabinet with screws. Install the drawer pulls and door knobs and you're finished.

tip Use dry graphite powder for lubricant in the tambour door tracks.

PROJECT EIGHT

freestanding bookcase

We can never have enough storage room —
it's a precious commodity. The bookcase in
this chapter is only 15" deep, so it will fit
neatly against a hallway wall or another area where
depth is limited. But it also has two large drawers for
some additional storage space.

This bookcase has room for four shelves that can
hold your favorite novels or decorative items. Its design is
in the Queen Anne style. It's built from poplar wood,
which makes this bookcase a useful and inexpensive way
to grab a little extra storage space.

This fun-to-build piece of furniture will help you
utilize space in a way you may not have thought of before.

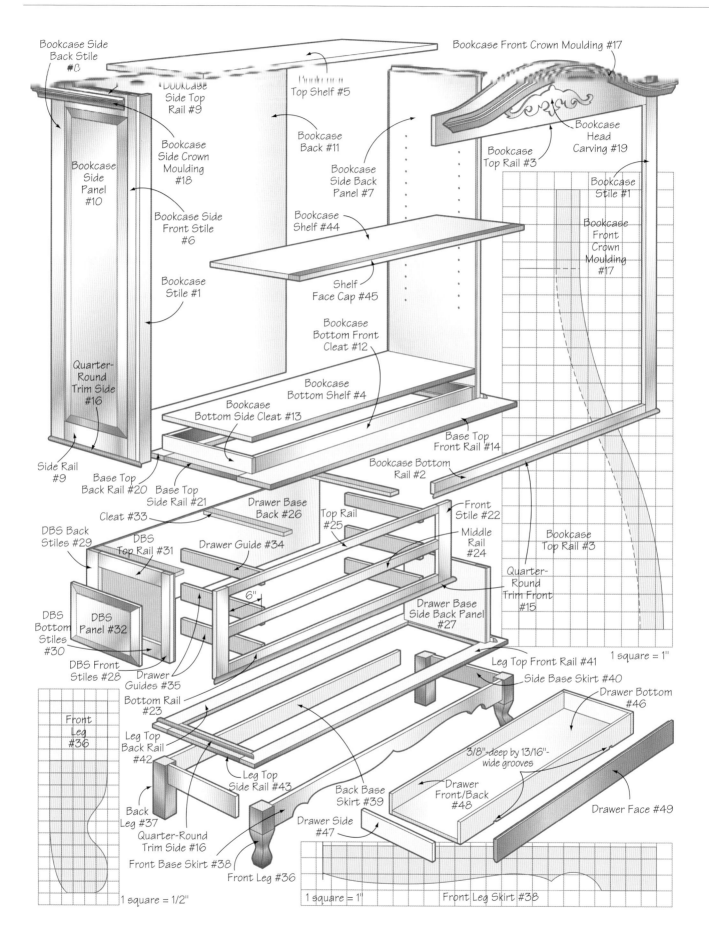

Bookcase Side Back Stile #8

Bookcase Side Top Rail #9

Bookcase Side Crown Moulding #18

Bookcase Side Panel #10

Bookcase Side Front Stile #6

Bookcase Stile #1

Quarter-Round Trim Side #16

Side Rail #9

Bookcase Top Shelf #5

Bookcase Back #11

Bookcase Side Back Panel #7

Bookcase Shelf #44

Shelf Face Cap #45

Bookcase Bottom Front Cleat #12

Bookcase Bottom Shelf #4

Bookcase Bottom Side Cleat #13

Bookcase Front Crown Moulding #17

Bookcase Head Carving #19

Bookcase Top Rail #3

Bookcase Stile #1

Bookcase Front Crown Moulding #17

Base Top Front Rail #14

Bookcase Bottom Rail #2

Base Top Back Rail #20

Base Top Side Rail #21

Cleat #33

Drawer Base Back #26

Top Rail #25

Front Stile #22

Middle Rail #24

Bookcase Top Rail #3

DBS Back Stiles #29

DBS Top Rail #31

Drawer Guide #34

Quarter-Round Trim Front #15

DBS Bottom Stiles #30

DBS Panel #32

DBS Front Stiles #28

Drawer Guides #35

6"

Drawer Base Side Back Panel #27

Leg Top Front Rail #41

Side Base Skirt #40

Drawer Bottom #46

Bottom Rail #23

Front Leg #36

Leg Top Back Rail #42

Back Leg #37

Quarter-Round Trim Side #16

Front Base Skirt #38

Leg Top Side Rail #43

Front Leg #36

Back Base Skirt #39

Drawer Side #47

1 square = 1"

3/8"-deep by 13/16"-wide grooves

Drawer Front/Back #48

Drawer Face #49

1 square = 1/2"

1 square = 1"

Front Leg Skirt #38

cutting list INCHES

REFERENCE	QUANTITY	PART	STOCK	THICKNESS	WIDTH	LENGTH	COMMENTS
1	2	Bookcase Stiles	Poplar	$3/4$	2	53	
2	1	Bookcase Bottom Rail	Poplar	$3/4$	$1^1/2$	41	
3	1	Bookcase Top Rail	Poplar	$3/4$	$8^1/2$	41	
4	1	Bookcase Bottom Shelf	Birch Ply.	$3/4$	10	43	
5	1	Bookcase Top Shelf	Birch Ply.	$3/4$	10	$43^1/2$	
6	2	Bookcase Side Front Stiles	Poplar	$3/4$	$1^1/4$	53	
7	2	Bookcase Side Back Panels	Birch Ply.	$1/4$	$10^1/4$	$52^1/4$	
8	2	Bookcase Side Back Stiles	Poplar	$3/4$	2	53	
9	4	Bookcase Side Top & Bottom Rails	Poplar	$3/4$	$3^1/4$	7	
10	2	Bookcase Side Inset Panels	Poplar	$3/4$	7	$46^1/2$	
11	1	Bookcase Back	Birch Ply.	$1/4$	45	53	
12	2	Bookcase Bottom Front Cleats	Any	$3/4$	$3/4$	43	
13	2	Bookcase Bottom Side Cleats	Any	$3/4$	$3/4$	$8^1/2$	
14	1	Base Top Front Rail	Poplar	$3/4$	5	50	
15	2	Quarter-Round Trim Front	Poplar	$1/2$	$1/2$	51	A
16	4	Quarter-Round Trim Sides	Poplar	$1/2$	$1/2$	16	A
17	1	Bookcase Front Crown Moulding	Poplar	$1^1/4$	$6^1/2$	50	B
18	2	Bookcase Side Crown Moulding	Poplar	$1^1/4$	$1^1/4$	14	B
19	1	Bookcase Head Carving	Birch	$1/4$	3	12	C
20	1	Base Top Back Rail	Poplar	$3/4$	$2^1/2$	50	
21	2	Base Top Side Rails	Poplar	$3/4$	$3^1/2$	$7^1/2$	
22	2	Drawer Base Front Stiles	Poplar	$3/4$	2	$14^1/2$	
23	1	Drawer Base Bottom Rail	Poplar	$3/4$	$1^3/4$	44	
24	1	Drawer Base Middle Rail	Poplar	$3/4$	$1^1/2$	44	
25	1	Drawer Base Top Rail	Poplar	$3/4$	$1^1/4$	44	
26	1	Drawer Base Back	Birch Ply.	$3/4$	$14^1/2$	$45^7/8$	
27	2	Drawer Base Side Back Panels	Birch Ply.	$1/4$	$13^1/4$	$14^1/2$	
28	2	Drawer Base Side Front Stiles	Poplar	$3/4$	$1^1/4$	$14^1/2$	
29	2	Drawer Base Side Back Stiles	Poplar	$3/4$	2	$14^1/2$	
30	2	Drawer Base Side Bottom Rails	Poplar	$3/4$	$3^1/4$	10	
31	2	Drawer Base Side Top Rails	Poplar	$3/4$	2	10	
32	2	Drawer Base Side Inset Panels	Poplar	$3/4$	$9^1/4$	10	
33	3	Drawer Base to Bookcase Cleats	Poplar	$3/4$	2	14	
34	2	Top Drawer Guides	Poplar	$3/4$	$1^5/8$	14	
35	4	Middle & Bottom Drawer Guides	Poplar	$3/4$	$2^1/4$	14	
36	2	Front Legs	Poplar	$2^1/2$	$2^1/2$	8	D
37	2	Back Legs	Poplar	$2^1/2$	$2^1/2$	8	
38	1	Front Base Skirt	Poplar	$3/4$	$2^3/4$	$43^1/8$	E
39	1	Back Base Skirt	Poplar	$3/4$	$2^3/4$	$43^1/8$	
40	2	Side Base Skirts	Poplar	$3/4$	$2^3/4$	$9^1/8$	
41	1	Leg Top Front Rail	Poplar	$3/4$	$3^1/2$	50	
42	1	Leg Top Back Rail	Poplar	$3/4$	$2^1/2$	50	
43	2	Leg Top Side Rails	Poplar	$3/4$	$3^1/2$	9	
44	4	Bookcase Shelves	Birch Ply.	$3/4$	$8^7/8$	43	
45	4	Bookcase Shelves' Face Caps	Poplar	$3/4$	1	43	
46	2	Drawer Bottoms	Melamine	$3/4$	$11^1/2$	$42^3/4$	
47	4	Drawer Sides	Melamine	$1/2$	$4^1/2$	$12^1/2$	
48	4	Drawer Fronts & Backs	Melamine	$1/2$	$4^1/2$	$42^3/4$	
49	2	Drawer Faces	Poplar	$3/4$	$5^1/2$	$44^1/2$	

A: Cut to fit on 45°

B: Cut to fit on 45°; glue two $3/4$" pieces together and rip to $1^1/4$"

C: Purchase at local home-improvement store

D: Refer to page 18 for cutting details

E: Cut to design

HARDWARE:

12' of $5/8$"-wide edge-banding tape to match color of melamine

4 drawer pulls

16 -$1/4$" shelf supports

cutting list MILLIMETERS

REFERENCE	QUANTITY	PART	STOCK	THICKNESS	WIDTH	LENGTH	COMMENTS
1	2	Bookcase Stiles	Poplar	19	51	1346	
2	1	Bookcase Bottom Rail	Poplar	19	38	1041	
3	1	Bookcase Top Rail	Poplar	19	216	1041	
4	1	Bookcase Bottom Shelf	Birch Ply.	19	254	1092	
5	1	Bookcase Top Shelf	Birch Ply.	19	254	1105	
6	2	Bookcase Side Front Stiles	Poplar	19	32	1346	
7	2	Bookcase Side Back Panels	Birch Ply.	6	260	1326	
8	2	Bookcase Side Back Stiles	Poplar	19	51	1346	
9	4	Bookcase Side Top & Bottom Rails	Poplar	19	82	178	
10	2	Bookcase Side Inset Panels	Poplar	19	178	1181	
11	1	Bookcase Back	Birch Ply.	6	1143	1346	
12	2	Bookcase Bottom Front Cleats	Any	19	19	1092	
13	2	Bookcase Bottom Side Cleats	Any	19	19	216	
14	1	Base Top Front Rail	Poplar	19	127	1270	
15	2	Quarter-Round Trim Front	Poplar	13	13	1295	A
16	4	Quarter-Round Trim Sides	Poplar	13	13	406	A
17	1	Bookcase Front Crown Moulding	Poplar	32	165	1270	B
18	2	Bookcase Side Crown Moulding	Poplar	32	32	356	B
19	1	Bookcase Head Carving	Birch	6	76	305	C
20	1	Base Top Back Rails	Poplar	19	64	1270	
21	2	Base Top Side Rails	Poplar	19	89	191	
22	2	Drawer Base Front Stiles	Poplar	19	51	369	
23	1	Drawer Base Bottom Rail	Poplar	19	45	1118	
24	1	Drawer Base Middle Rail	Poplar	19	38	1118	
25	1	Drawer Base Top Rail	Poplar	19	32	1118	
26	1	Drawer Base Back	Birch Ply.	19	369	1165	
27	2	Drawer Base Side Back Panels	Birch Ply.	6	336	369	
28	2	Drawer Base Side Front Stiles	Poplar	19	32	369	
29	2	Drawer Base Side Back Stiles	Poplar	19	51	369	
30	2	Drawer Base Side Bottom Rails	Poplar	19	82	254	
31	2	Drawer Base Side Top Rails	Poplar	19	51	254	
32	2	Drawer Base Side Inset Panels	Poplar	19	235	254	
33	3	Drawer Base to Bookcase Cleats	Poplar	19	51	356	
34	2	Top Drawer Guides	Poplar	19	41	356	
35	4	Middle & Bottom Drawer Guides	Poplar	19	57	356	
36	2	Front Legs	Poplar	64	64	203	D
37	2	Back Legs	Poplar	64	64	203	
38	1	Front Base Skirt	Poplar	19	70	1095	E
39	1	Back Base Skirt	Poplar	19	70	1095	
40	2	Sides Base Skirt	Poplar	19	70	232	
41	1	Leg Top Front Rail	Poplar	19	89	1270	
42	1	Leg Top Back Rail	Poplar	19	64	1270	
43	2	Leg Top Side Rails	Poplar	19	89	229	
44	4	Bookcase Shelves	Birch Ply.	19	225	1092	
45	4	Bookcase Shelves' Face Caps	Poplar	19	25	1092	
46	2	Drawer Bottoms	Melamine	19	292	1086	
47	4	Drawer Sides	Melamine	13	115	318	
48	4	Drawer Fronts & Backs	Melamine	13	115	1086	
49	2	Drawer Faces	Poplar	19	140	1131	

A: Cut to fit on 45°

B: Cut to fit on 45°; glue two 19 mm pieces together and rip to 32 mm

C: Purchase at local home-improvement store

D: Refer to page 18 for cutting details

E: Cut to design

HARDWARE:

3.5m of 16mm-wide edge-banding tape to match color of melamine

4 drawer pulls

16 - 6 mm shelf supports

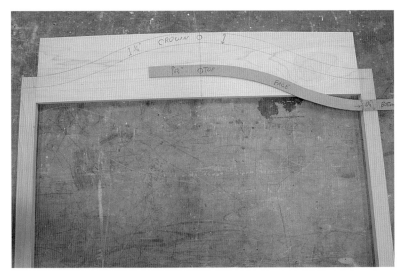

1. Assemble the bookcase face frame. Hold down the bookcase top rail 3¼" into the side stiles. Make a template for the crown moulding and trace the pattern onto the face frame.

2. Use your jigsaw to cut the top of the crown moulding arch.

3. Assemble the side panels (see "Alternative Woodworking Techniques" pages 9-10). Use your table saw to cut a ¼" × ½" notch into the inside back of the side panels. This notch will receive the ¼" back panel.

4 | Assemble the bookcase with glue and nails. Then, nail the ¼" back panel into the notch in the back of the bookcase.

5 | Make a drilling jig out of scrap wood with ¼" holes drilled 2" apart for the adjustable shelf supports. Use this jig to drill the holes ⅜"-deep into the sides of the bookcase. Be careful when you drill the shelf holes to not drill through the thin part of the side insert panel.

6 | Make the bookcase crown moulding by cutting two ¾" × 6½" × 50" pieces into the crown moulding shape using your crown moulding pattern. Then glue and clamp together as needed. Do not use nails. After the glue has dried, turn the moulding upside down and cut it to 1¼" thick with your table saw.

7 Sand the inside of the crown moulding smooth with your drill and sanding drum.

8 Set your table saw blade to 45°. Set your miter gauge to 90° and use a straightedge to cut the crown moulding on a 45° angle to fit the bookcase.

9 Glue the crown moulding onto the face frame. (Do not use nails.) Then, use your router and a ½" cove router bit to rout the crown moulding using two different settings. First, cut the lower cove. This is a deep cut, so you might want to make it in two shallower cuts. Be careful to not touch the bookcase face frame with the router bit. Then, lower the router base (which "raises" the bit), and make the second cove cut. This cut is much shallower than the first. Using this method is a simple but effective way to make an attractive moulding. (See photo #12 for a detail of the finished crown moulding.)

10 An inexpensive nice touch to add is a decorative woodcarving. You can purchase one at any local home-improvement store. Attach it with glue and hold it in place with masking tape until the glue sets up.

11 Assemble the base top frame (see "Alternative Woodworking Methods" on pages 9-10). Attach the base top assembly to the bookcase bottom with 1½" screws. Then, use a ¼" roundover router bit in your router and cut the roundover on the sides and front top and bottom edges.

12 Rout the outside edges of the bookcase face frame with your router and a ¼" roundover bit. This is a stopped cut at the bottom and top of the face frame. Use the base top assembly as a stop for the router at the bottom and the crown moulding as a stop at the top of the upper cabinet.

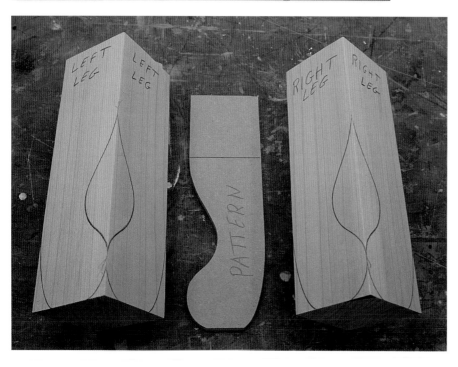

13 Make a leg pattern and trace the shape onto two sides of the front legs as shown.

14 Use your pattern to set the table-saw blade height and the fence, then cut out the design on the two outside portions of the two front legs. Repeat this process to cut out the two inside portions of the two front legs. Adjust the blade and fence as needed. Then, sand out the saw marks on the legs to a smooth finish using your drill and sanding drum.

15 Cut and sand the design on the front leg skirt. Then, glue the legs and leg skirts together, creating the leg assembly. Hold the leg skirts ³⁄₈" inside of the outside edges of the legs.

16 Assemble the leg top frame. (See step #11 in this chapter.) Screw the leg top assembly to the leg assembly with 1¹⁄₂" screws.

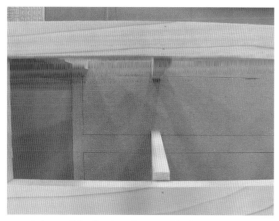

17 Assemble the face frame with dowels and glue. Before you assemble the drawer base body, trace the face frame onto the drawer base back. Then assemble the body. Install the drawer guides 6" in from each side using the lines on the drawer base back to align the guides.

18 Screw the leg assembly to the drawer base body with 1¼" screws.

19 Cut out the drawer parts. Center the drawer bottoms in the drawer openings and trace the drawer guides onto the drawer bottoms.

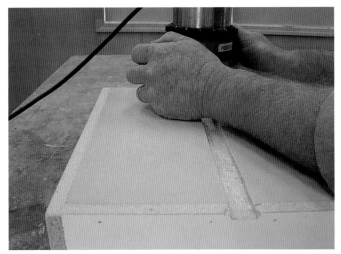

20 Assemble the drawers, then use your router and a ½" straight bit to rout two ⅜"-deep by ¹³⁄₁₆"-wide drawer tracks on each drawer bottom. You can also use your table saw to cut these grooves.

21 Screw the drawer base assembly to the bookcase with 1½" screws.

22 When you make the shelves, glue a ¾" × 1" face cap onto the shelves to hide the veneered edge of the plywood. Sand the face cap flush with the plywood. (Be careful to not sand through the plywood veneer when you sand the face cap.) Then, use your router and a ¼" roundover bit to round over the top and bottom edges of the face cap.

23 By using poplar to build this project, I saved money on materials costs. After the project was finished sanded, I used a dark cherry stain to color the wood and applied the finish coat. This project came out looking exactly like cherry wood. It worked even better than I had hoped!

hall tree seat

Most homes have an empty space by the front door; if yours does, here is a good use for that space.

This hall tree seat has two hooks for you to hang your coat or scarf on when you come in from the cool night air. It also has a mirror so you can check that everything is in place before you head back out.

This project has a large storage area under the seat in which you can store boots, gloves or just extra things. This project will make a nice addition to any home.

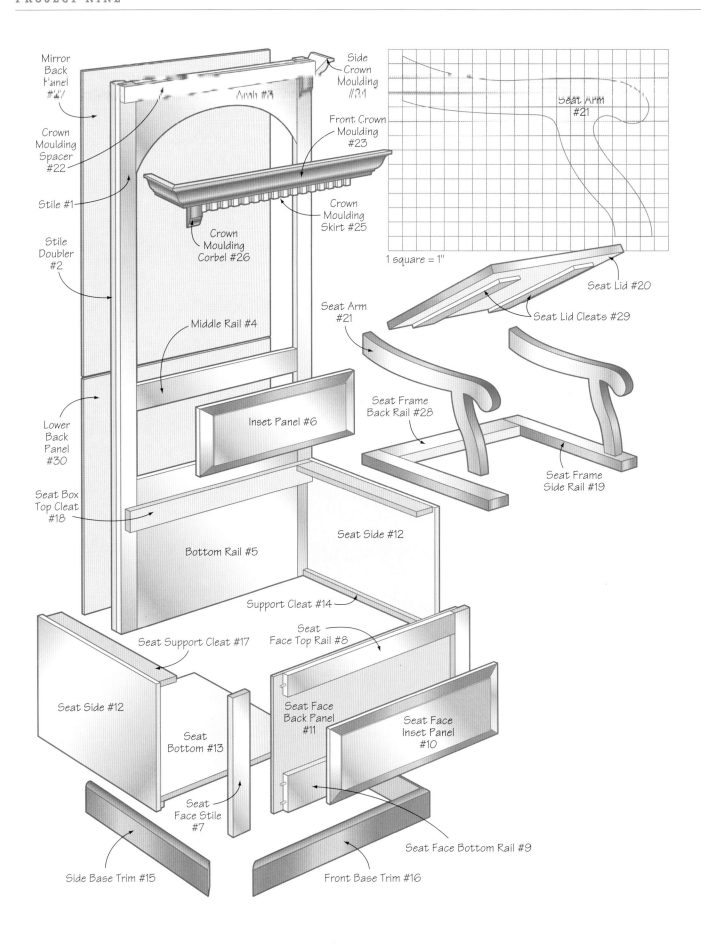

Mirror Back Panel #27

Crown Moulding Spacer #22

Stile #1

Stile Doubler #2

Lower Back Panel #30

Seat Box Top Cleat #18

Side Crown Moulding #31

Front Crown Moulding #23

Crown Moulding Skirt #25

Crown Moulding Corbel #26

Arch #3

Middle Rail #4

Inset Panel #6

Bottom Rail #5

Seat Support Cleat #17

Seat Side #12

Seat Bottom #13

Seat Face Stile #7

Side Base Trim #15

Seat Arm #21

1 square = 1"

Seat Lid #20

Seat Lid Cleats #29

Seat Arm #21

Seat Frame Back Rail #28

Seat Frame Side Rail #19

Seat Side #12

Support Cleat #14

Seat Face Top Rail #8

Seat Face Back Panel #11

Seat Face Inset Panel #10

Seat Face Bottom Rail #9

Front Base Trim #16

cutting list INCHES

REFERENCE	QUANTITY	PART	STOCK	THICKNESS	WIDTH	LENGTH	COMMENTS
1	2	Hall Tree Stiles	Pine	3/4	4	78	
2	2	Hall Tree Stile Doublers	Pine	3/4	2^{11}/16	78	
3	1	Hall Tree Arch	Pine	3/4	19	23^3/8	
4	1	Hall Tree Middle Rail	Pine	3/4	3	23^3/8	
5	1	Hall Tree Bottom Rail	Pine	3/4	21^3/4	23^3/8	
6	1	Hall Tree Inset Panel	Pine	3/4	10^7/8	23^3/8	
7	2	Seat Face Stiles	Pine	3/4	3	17^1/4	
8	1	Seat Face Top Rail	Pine	3/4	2^1/2	22^3/8	
9	1	Seat Face Bottom Rail	Pine	3/4	5^3/4	22^3/8	
10	1	Seat Face Inset Panel	Pine	3/4	9^1/16	22^3/8	
11	1	Seat Face Back Panel	Plywood	1/4	17^1/4	26^{13}/16	
12	2	Seat Sides	Pine	3/4	17^1/4	17	
13	1	Seat Bottom	Pine	3/4	16^3/4	26^{13}/16	
14	2	Seat Bottom Support Cleats	Pine	3/4	2	16^3/4	
15	2	Base Trim Sides	Pine	3/4	3^1/2	22	A
16	1	Base Trim Front	Pine	3/4	3^1/2	33	A
17	2	Seat Support Cleats	Pine	3/4	2^1/2	16	
18	1	Seat Box Top Cleat	Pine	3/4	2	26^{13}/16	
19	2	Seat Frame Side Rails	Pine	1^1/2	3^1/4	18^1/2	
20	1	Seat Lid	Pine	1^1/2	15^1/4	23^1/4	
21	2	Seat Arms	Pine	1^1/2	15^1/4	25^1/2	B
22	1	Crown Moulding Spacer	Pine	3/4	3	31^3/8	
23	1	Crown Moulding Front	Pine	1/2	3^1/2	36	C
24	2	Crown Moulding Sides	Pine	1/2	3^1/2	12	C
25	1	Crown Moulding Skirt	Pine	3/4	1^1/8	24^7/8	
26	2	Crown Moulding Corbels	Pine	5/8	2^1/2	3(tall)	D
27	1	Mirror Back Panel	Plywood	1/4	25^7/8	44	
28	1	Seat Frame Back Rail	Pine	1^1/2	3^1/4	23^3/8	
29	2	Seat Lid Cleats	Pine	3/4	2^1/2	13^1/8	
30	1	Lower Back Panel	Plywood	1/4	25^7/8	34	

A: Cut to fit*

B: Cut to design

C: Purchase at home-improvement store

D: With router cut of your choice at bottom

HARDWARE:

2 coat hooks

1 beveled-edge arched mirror, 3/16" x 24" x 36"; purchase at home-improvement store before beginning this project, then fit the hall tree to the beveled-edge arched mirror (this is a lot easier than having a beveled-edge arched mirror cut to size)

2 flat seat hinges

cutting list MILLIMETERS

REFERENCE	QUANTITY	PART	STOCK	THICKNESS	WIDTH	LENGTH	COMMENTS
1	2	Hall Tree Stiles	Pine	19	102	1981	
2	2	Hall Tree Stiles Doubler	Pine	19	69	1981	
3	1	Hall Tree Arch	Pine	19	483	594	
4	1	Hall Tree Middle Rail	Pine	19	76	594	
5	1	Hall Tree Bottom Rail	Pine	19	552	594	
6	1	Hall Tree Inset Panel	Pine	19	276	594	
7	2	Seat Face Stiles	Pine	19	76	438	
8	1	Seat Face Top Rail	Pine	19	64	569	
9	1	Seat Face Bottom Rail	Pine	19	146	569	
10	1	Seat Face Inset Panel	Pine	19	231	569	
11	1	Seat Face Back Panel	Plywood	6	438	681	
12	2	Seat Sides	Pine	19	438	432	
13	1	Seat Bottom	Pine	19	425	681	
14	2	Seat Bottom Support Cleats	Pine	19	51	425	
15	2	Base Trim Sides	Pine	19	89	559	A
16	1	Base Trim Front	Pine	19	89	838	A
17	2	Seat Support Cleats	Pine	19	64	406	
18	1	Seat Box Top Cleat	Pine	19	51	681	
19	2	Seat Frame Side Rail	Pine	38	82	470	
20	1	Seat Lid	Pine	38	387	590	
21	2	Seat Arms	Pine	38	387	648	B
22	1	Crown Moulding Spacer	Pine	19	76	797	
23	1	Crown Moulding Front	Pine	13	89	914	C
24	2	Crown Moulding Sides	Pine	13	89	305	C
25	1	Crown Moulding Skirt	Pine	19	29	632	
26	2	Crown Moulding Corbels	Pine	16	64	76(tall)	D
27	1	Mirror Back Panel	Plywood	6	657	1118	
28	1	Seat Frame Back Rail	Pine	38	82	594	
29	2	Seat Lid Cleats	Pine	19	64	333	
30	1	Lower Back Panel	Plywood	6	657	864	

A: Cut to fit*

B: Cut to design

C: Purchase at home-improvement store

D: With router cut of your choice at bottom

HARDWARE:

2 coat hooks

1 beveled-edge arched mirror, 5mm x 610mm x 914mm; purchase at home-improvement store before beginning this project, then fit the hall tree to the beveled-edge arched mirror (this is a lot easier than having a beveled-edge arched mirror cut to size)

2 flat seat hinges

1 Make the storage seat parts and cut them per the cutting list. Then, glue and nail the storage seat assembly together.

2 Make the seat face panel assembly (see "Alternative Woodworking Techniques" on pages 9-10). Nail and glue the face panel assembly to the front of the storage seat. Use clamps to hold the face panel snug until the glue is dry. Next, install the seat support cleats and the seat box top cleat.

3 Assemble the back frame of the hall tree, then lay a 24" × 36" arched mirror on the back of the hall tree frame. Trace the mirror. Note: The mirror can be purchased at any local home-improvement store. It's cheaper to buy a factory-cut arched mirror than to have one cut to fit.

4   Use a ⅜" spacer to draw a line on the inside of the traced mirror line. This is the line you will follow and cut with your jigsaw.

5   Cut out the arch, then use your drill and sanding drum to sand the inside of the arch smooth.

6   Rout a ⅜"-wide by ¼"-deep notch on the back of the mirrored opening with a ⅜" rabbeting bit. Use your hammer and chisel to square the routed corners.

7 Glue and nail on the hall tree stile doublers, then glue and nail on the lower ¼" back panel.

8 Set your table saw blade to 45° and the miter gauge to 90°. Pretend the saw table is the back of the hall tree and the miter gauge is the top. Cut the crown moulding to fit the hall tree back. Attach the crown moulding to the front top of the hall tree with glue and nails. The top of the moulding is held flush with the top of the hall tree.

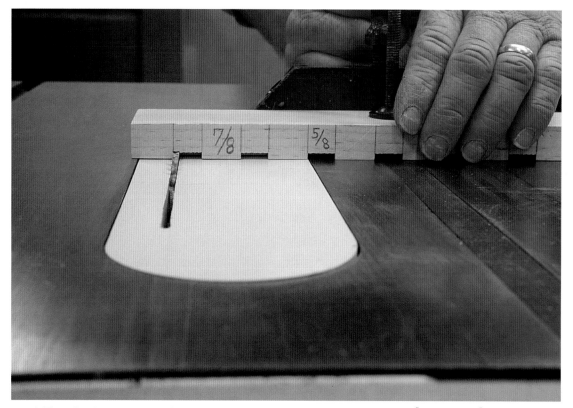

9 To make the crown moulding skirt, lay out the skirt starting at one end with ⅞" and then ⅝". Repeat this process all the way along the skirt, finishing with ⅞". Set your table saw blade ³⁄₁₆" high, and using your miter gauge, dado the ⅝" portions of the skirt.

10 Center the crown moulding skirt under the crown moulding spacer. Glue and nail it on. Make the corbels by routing an ogee profile on one edge of a ¾"-thick by 3"-wide by 12"-long piece of pine. (This will give you plenty of material to cut the corbels.) Crosscut two 2½"-wide corbels. Then glue and nail the crown moulding corbels tightly against the crown moulding spacer and the crown moulding skirt.

11 Use your router and a ½" roundover bit to round over the front sides of the hall tree back. Let the router base touch the crown moulding corbels and rout all the way to the bottom.

12 Screw the hall tree back to the back of the storage seat with 2½" wood screws.

13 | Attach the base trim onto the storage seat. Round over the two front edges of the storage seat with a ½" roundover bit, allowing the router base to touch the base trim as a stop.

14 | Make the seat frame and attach it temporarily to the storage seat with 1½" screws.

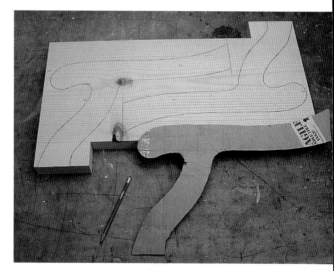

15 | Make an arm pattern from cardboard and use it to trace the arms onto the arm stock. Hold the bottom of the arm pattern flush with the bottom of the arm stock. This will create a 90° angle where the back of the arm meets the seat.

16 Cut out the arms using your jigsaw, then sand the outside portions with your belt sander.

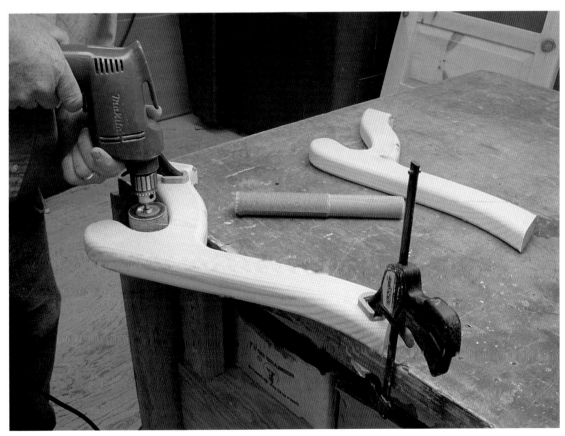

17 Sand the inside portions of the arms with your drill and drum sander.

18 Round over all the edges of both arms with your router and a ¹⁄₂" roundover bit. Be sure to leave the ends square that attach to the back and seat. (A piece of scrap carpet pad makes a great routing pad.)

19 Hold the arms in place and trace the ends onto the seat frame and back of the hall tree.

20 Predrill screw holes through the hall tree back. Then remove the seat frame assembly and predrill screw holes through the seat frame. Locate the holes so the screws will not protrude from the arms.

21 Screw the arms onto the seat frame assembly with 2½" screws, then re-install the seat frame assembly onto the storage seat. Then screw the arms to the hall tree back with 2½" screws.

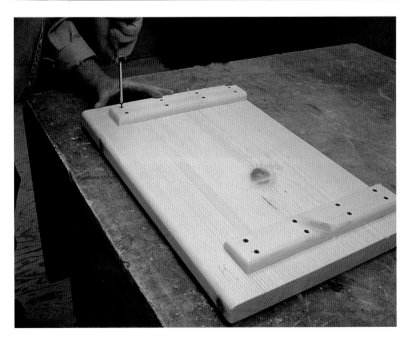

22 Make the seat lid. Round over the top and bottom of the front edge of the lid using a ½" round over bit and your router. Then, screw the seat lid cleats onto the bottom of the seat with 1½" screws. Finish sand all the parts. I used a light brown wood stain, then applied the finish. Put the lid in place and attach the hinges on top of the seat frame back rail and the lid. Install the mirror using a bead of silicone adhesive in the rabbet that will hold the mirror. Gently press the mirror in place and install the back with screws. Let the silicone cure before moving the hall tree. Attach a couple of coat hooks on the hall tree back stiles.

PROJECT TEN

built-in bookcase

Sometimes, a freestanding piece of furniture is just not what you're looking for. This was the case at Ron and Fran Stolich's home. Fran wanted a large bookcase, with large storage spaces underneath, that would blend with the house and wouldn't be intrusive. This bookcase was designed to match an existing bookcase already in their home.

The bookcase has two center shelves, with the center bay larger than the top and bottom bays. This makes for a unique display area. It has four large storage compartments in the bottom, and three center drawers. The bookcase top trim profile matches the existing door trim in their home.

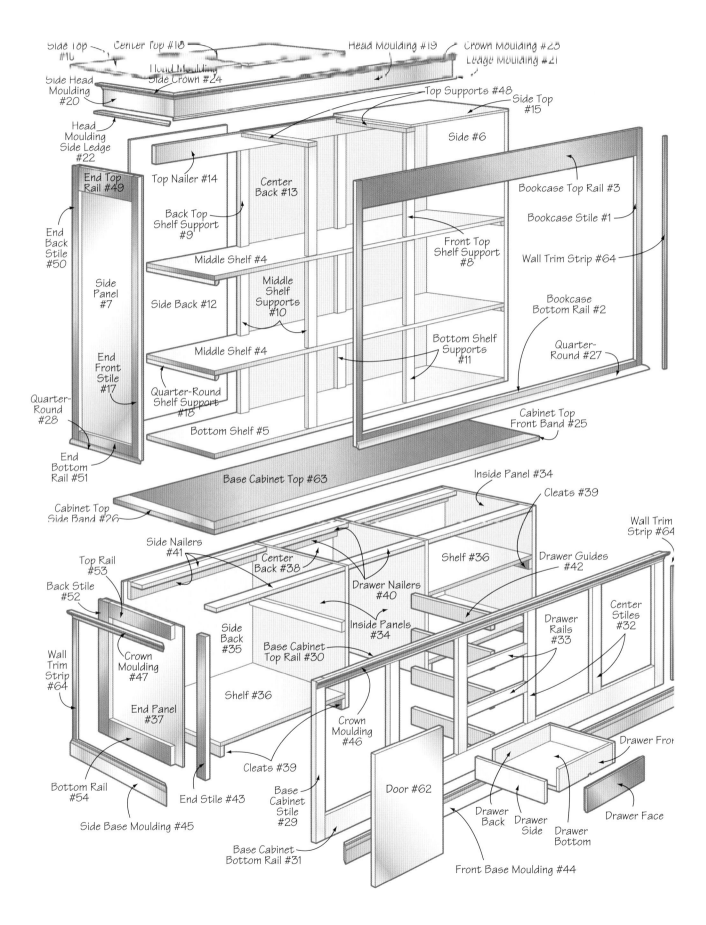

Side Top #16

Center Top #18

Head Moulding #19

Crown Moulding #23

Ledge Moulding #21

Side Head Moulding #20

Head Moulding Side Crown #24

Head Moulding Side Ledge #22

Top Supports #48

Side Top #15

Side #6

End Top Rail #49

Top Nailer #14

Center Back #13

Bookcase Top Rail #3

End Back Stile #50

Back Top Shelf Support #9

Bookcase Stile #1

Side Panel #7

Middle Shelf #4

Front Top Shelf Support #8

Wall Trim Strip #64

Middle Shelf Supports #10

Side Back #12

End Front Stile #17

Middle Shelf #4

Bookcase Bottom Rail #2

Quarter-Round #27

Quarter-Round #28

Quarter-Round Shelf Support #18

Bottom Shelf Supports #11

Bottom Shelf #5

Cabinet Top Front Band #25

End Bottom Rail #51

Base Cabinet Top #63

Inside Panel #34

Cleats #39

Cabinet Top Side Band #26

Side Nailers #41

Center Back #38

Shelf #36

Drawer Guides #42

Wall Trim Strip #64

Top Rail #53

Drawer Nailers #40

Back Stile #52

Inside Panels #34

Drawer Rails #33

Center Stiles #32

Wall Trim Strip #64

Crown Moulding #47

Side Back #35

Base Cabinet Top Rail #30

End Panel #37

Shelf #36

Crown Moulding #46

Door #62

Drawer Front

Bottom Rail #54

End Stile #43

Base Cabinet Stile #29

Drawer Back

Drawer Side

Drawer Bottom

Drawer Face

Side Base Moulding #45

Base Cabinet Bottom Rail #31

Front Base Moulding #44

Cleats #39

cutting list INCHES

REFERENCE	QUANTITY	PART	STOCK	THICKNESS	WIDTH	LENGTH	COMMENTS
1	2	Bookcase Stiles	Poplar	3/4	1 3/4	56 1/4	
2	1	Bookcase Bottom Rail	Poplar	3/4	2	100	
3	1	Bookcase Top Rail	Poplar	3/4	7 3/4	100	
4	2	Bookcase Middle Shelves	Birch Ply.*	3/4	12 1/4	101 3/8	A
5	1	Bookcase Bottom Shelf	Birch Ply.	3/4	12 1/4	101 3/8	
6	1	Bookcase Side	Birch Ply.	3/4	12 1/4	56 1/4	
7	1	Bookcase Side Panel	Birch Ply.	1/4	12 1/4	56 1/4	
8	2	Front Top Shelf Supports	Poplar	3/4	1 1/2	20	
9	2	Back Top Shelf Supports	Poplar	3/4	1 1/2	18 1/4	
10	4	Middle Shelf Supports	Poplar	3/4	1 1/2	17	
11	4	Bottom Shelf Supports	Poplar	3/4	1 1/2	14	
12	2	Bookcase Backs (Sides)	Birch Ply.	1/4	34 3/4	56 1/4	
13	1	Bookcase Back (Center)	Birch Ply.	1/4	33 1/2	56 1/4	
14	1	Bookcase Top Nailer	Poplar	3/4	3 1/2	101 3/8	
15	2	Bookcase Tops (Sides)	Birch Ply.	1/4	13	34 3/4	
16	1	Bookcase Top (Center)	Birch Ply.	1/4	13	33 1/2	
17	1	Bookcase End Stile (Front)	Poplar	3/4	1 1/4	56 1/4	
18	4	Quarter-Round Shelf Supports	Poplar	1/2	1/2	12 1/4	
19	1	Head Moulding (Front)	Poplar	3/4	5 1/2	106	B
20	1	Head Moulding (Side)	Poplar	3/4	5 1/2	16	B
21	1	Head Moulding Ledge (Front)	Poplar	3/8	1 1/4	106	B
22	1	Head Moulding Ledge (Side)	Poplar	3/8	1 1/4	16	B
23	1	Head Crown Moulding (Front)	Pine	1/2	1 5/8	106	B
24	1	Head Crown Moulding (Side)	Pine	1/2	1 5/8	16	B
25	1	Base Cabinet Top Band (Front)	Poplar	3/4	1	108	B
26	1	Base Cabinet Top Band (Side)	Poplar	3/4	1	20	B
27	1	Quarter-Round Bookcase Trim	Poplar	1/2	1/2	106	B
28	1	Quarter-Round Bookcase Trim	Poplar	1/2	1/2	16	B
29	2	Base Cabinet Stiles	Poplar	3/4	2	29 1/2	
30	1	Base Cabinet Top Rail	Poplar	3/4	2 1/2	100 1/2	
31	1	Base Cabinet Bottom Rail	Poplar	3/4	5	100 1/2	
32	4	Base Cabinet Center Stiles	Poplar	3/4	2	22	
33	2	Base Cabinet Drawer Rails	Poplar	3/4	2	18 1/2	
34	3	Base Cabinet Inside Panels	Birch Ply.	3/4	16 1/4	29 1/2	
35	2	Base Cabinet Back (Sides)	Birch Ply.	1/4	25 3/8	42 1/4	
36	4	Base Cabinet Bottom & Shelves	Birch Ply.	3/4	16 1/4	41 1/8	
37	1	Base Cabinet End Back Panel	Birch Ply.	1/4	16 1/4	29 1/2	
38	1	Base Cabinet Back (Center)	Birch Ply.	1/4	19 1/4	29 1/4	
39	8	Bottom & Shelf Cleats	Poplar	3/4	1 1/4	16 1/4	
40	3	Base Cabinet Drawer Nailers	Any	3/4	3 1/2	18 1/2	
41	6	Base Cabinet Side Nailers	Any	3/4	3 1/2	41 1/8	
42	4	Drawer Guides	Poplar	3/4	2 3/4	16 1/4	
43	2	Base Cabinet End Stiles (Front)	Poplar	3/4	1/4	29 1/2	
44	1	Base Cabinet Base Moulding (Front)	Poplar	3/4	3 1/2	108	B
45	1	Base Cabinet Base Moulding (Side)	Poplar	3/4	3 1/2	20	B
46	1	Base Cabinet Crown Moulding (Front)	Pine	1/2	1 5/8	108	B
47	1	Base Cabinet Crown Moulding (Side)	Pine	1/2	1 5/8	20	B
48	2	Bookcase Top Supports	Poplar	3/4	1 1/2	11 1/2	
49	1	Bookcase End Top Rail	Poplar	3/4	7 3/4	9	
50	1	Bookcase End Stile (Back)	Poplar	3/4	2	56 1/4	
51	1	Bookcase End Bottom Rail	Poplar	3/4	2	9	
52	1	Base Cabinet End Stile (Back)	Poplar	3/4	2	29 1/2	
53	1	Base Cabinet End Top Rail	Poplar	3/4	4 1/4	13	
54	1	Base Cabinet End Bottom Rail	Poplar	3/4	7	13	
55	3	Drawer Bottoms	Melamine	3/4	14 1/2	17 1/4	
56	4	Drawer Sides (Top & Middle)	Melamine	1/2	4 1/2	15 1/2	
57	2	Drawer Sides (Bottom)	Melamine	1/2	7 1/2	15 1/2	
58	4	Drawer Sides (Top & Middle)	Melamine	1/2	4 1/2	17 1/4	
59	2	Drawer Sides (Bottom)	Melamine	1/2	7 1/2	17 1/4	
60	2	Drawer Face (Top & Middle)	Birch Ply.	3/4	5 1/2	19	
61	1	Drawer Face (Bottom)	Birch Ply.	3/4	8 1/2	19	
62	4	Base Cabinet Doors	Birch Ply.	3/4	19	22 1/2	
63	1	Base Cabinet Top	Birch Ply.	3/4	17 1/2	105	
64	2	Wall Trim Strips	Poplar	1/4	3/4	96	

*Plywood

A: Edge band middle shelves with 3/8" poplar

B: Cut 45° to fit at corner

HARDWARE:

20' of 5/8"-wide edge-banding to match color of melamine

50' of 13/16"-wide birch edge-banding tape

8 - 3/8" backset hinges

7 door and drawer pulls

cutting list MILLIMETERS

REFERENCE	QUANTITY	PART	STOCK	THICKNESS	WIDTH	LENGTH	COMMENTS
1	2	Bookcase Stiles	Poplar	19	45	1428	
2	1	Bookcase Bottom Rail	Poplar	19	51	2540	
3	1	Bookcase Top Rail	Poplar	19	197	2540	
4	2	Bookcase Middle Shelves	Birch Ply.*	19	311	2575	A
5	1	Bookcase Bottom Shelf	Birch Ply.	19	311	2575	
6	1	Bookcase Side	Birch Ply.	19	311	1428	
7	1	Bookcase Side Panel	Birch Ply.	6	311	1428	
8	2	Front Top Shelf Supports	Poplar	19	38	508	
9	2	Back Top Shelf Supports	Poplar	19	38	463	
10	4	Middle Shelf Supports	Poplar	19	38	432	
11	4	Bottom Shelf Supports	Poplar	19	38	356	
12	2	Bookcase Racks (Sides)	Birch Ply.	6	883	1428	
13	1	Bookcase Back (Center)	Birch Ply.	6	851	1428	
14	1	Bookcase Top Nailer	Poplar	19	89	2575	
15	2	Bookcase Tops (Sides)	Birch Ply.	6	330	883	
16	1	Bookcase Top (Center)	Birch Ply.	6	330	851	
17	1	Bookcase End Stile (Front)	Poplar	19	32	1428	
18	4	Quarter-Round Shelf Supports	Poplar	13	13	311	
19	1	Head Moulding (Front)	Poplar	19	140	2692	B
20	1	Head Moulding (Side)	Poplar	19	140	406	B
21	1	Head Moulding Ledge (Front)	Poplar	10	32	2692	B
22	1	Head Moulding Ledge (Side)	Poplar	10	32	406	B
23	1	Head Crown Moulding (Front)	Pine	13	41	2692	B
24	1	Head Crown Moulding (Side)	Pine	13	41	406	B
25	1	Base Cabinet Top Band (Front)	Poplar	19	25	2743	B
26	1	Base Cabinet Top Band (Side)	Poplar	19	25	508	B
27	1	Quarter-Round Bookcase Trim	Poplar	13	13	2692	B
28	1	Quarter-Round Bookcase Trim	Poplar	13	13	406	B
29	2	Base Cabinet Stiles	Poplar	19	51	750	
30	1	Base Cabinet Top Rail	Poplar	19	64	2553	
31	1	Base Cabinet Bottom Rail	Poplar	19	127	2553	
32	4	Base Cabinet Center Stiles	Poplar	19	51	559	
33	2	Base Cabinet Drawer Rails	Poplar	19	51	470	
34	3	Base Cabinet Inside Panels	Birch Ply.	19	412	750	
35	2	Base Cabinet Back (Sides)	Birch Ply.	6	645	1073	
36	4	Base Cabinet Bottom & Shelves	Birch Ply.	19	412	1044	
37	1	Base Cabinet End Back Panel	Birch Ply.	6	412	750	
38	1	Base Cabinet Back (Center)	Birch Ply.	6	489	743	
39	8	Bottom & Shelf Cleats	Poplar	19	32	412	
40	3	Base Cabinet Drawer Nailers	Any	19	89	470	
41	6	Base Cabinet Side Nailers	Any	19	89	1044	
42	4	Drawer Guides	Poplar	19	70	412	
43	2	Base Cabinet End Stiles (Front)	Poplar	19	6	750	
44	1	Base Cabinet Base Moulding (Front)	Poplar	19	89	2743	B
45	1	Base Cabinet Base Moulding (Side)	Poplar	19	89	508	B
46	1	Base Cabinet Crown Moulding (Front)	Pine	13	41	2743	B
47	1	Base Cabinet Crown Moulding (Side)	Pine	13	41	508	B
48	2	Bookcase Top Supports	Poplar	19	38	292	
49	1	Bookcase End Top Rail	Poplar	19	197	229	
50	1	Bookcase End Stile (Back)	Poplar	19	51	1428	
51	1	Bookcase End Bottom Rail	Poplar	19	51	229	
52	1	Base Cabinet End Stile (Back)	Poplar	19	51	750	
53	1	Base Cabinet End Top Rail	Poplar	19	108	330	
54	1	Base Cabinet End Bottom Rail	Poplar	19	178	330	
55	3	Drawer Bottoms	Melamine	19	369	438	
56	4	Drawer Sides (Top & Middle)	Melamine	13	115	394	
57	2	Drawer Sides (Bottom)	Melamine	13	191	394	
58	4	Drawer Sides (Top & Middle)	Melamine	13	115	438	
59	2	Drawer Sides (Bottom)	Melamine	13	191	438	
60	2	Drawer Faces (Top & Middle)	Birch Ply.	19	140	483	
61	1	Drawer Face (Bottom)	Birch Ply.	19	216	483	
62	4	Base Cabinet Doors	Birch Ply.	19	483	572	
63	1	Base Cabinet Top	Birch Ply.	19	445	2667	
64	2	Wall Trim Strips	Poplar	6	19	2438	

*Plywood

A: Edge band middle shelves with 10 mm poplar

B: Cut 45° to fit at corner

HARDWARE:

6m of 16mm-wide edge-banding to match color of melamine

15m of 21mm wide edge-banding tape

8 - 10 backset hinges

7-door and drawer pulls

1 | Sometimes the perfect location has obstacles in the way, such as the electric wall heater no longer in use. There were two logical choices before me when I designed this cabinet: Make the cabinet smaller so it doesn't interfere with the wall heater, or have the heater removed (by a qualified electrician) and make the cabinet long enough to cover the former heater location. Fran chose the latter because she wanted more storage space.

2 | The next step was to have the wall heater removed. Then, remove any baseboard trim where the bookcase will be located. Remove the carpet from the area where the bookcase will sit, so that the bookcase will sit solidly on the floor. If you choose to have any electrical outlets in the bookcase, have an electrician prewire in the wall behind the bookcase prior to installation.

3 | Assemble the lower face frame and the base cabinet bodies, then glue and nail the face frame to the bodies.

4 Clamp the face frame to the bodies as needed.

5 Glue and nail on the cleats to permanently support the bottom and shelf of the base cabinet.

6 Nail the ¼" back panel onto the base cabinet.

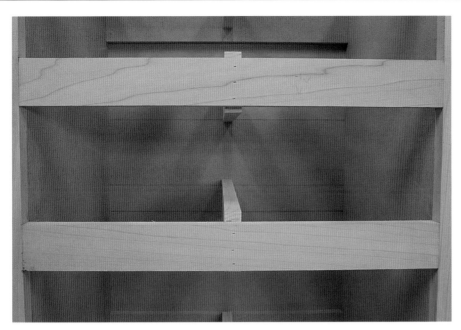

7 Install the drawer guides into the center of the drawer opening, level front to back. The drawer guides extend above and below the cabinet drawer rails ⅜".

8 Assemble the upper bookcase cabinet and face frame. Glue and nail the upper face frame onto the upper bookcase sides.

9 Glue and nail the center shelf supports into the upper cabinet to divide the bookcase into three equal parts. Nail the shelf supports flush to the front and back of the shelves.

10 Overlap the bookcase top rail 5" with the head moulding. Nail the bookcase head moulding on. Then cut and nail on the bookcase head moulding ledge.

11 Cut the head moulding crown to fit the head moulding. Use a scrap piece of wood as a guage and hold the top of the crown moulding flush with the top of the headmoulding. Glue and nail the crown moulding to the head moulding.

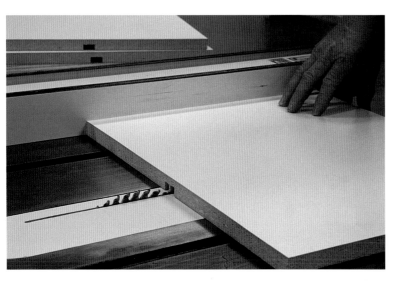

12 On the table saw, cut a $^{13}/_{16}$"-wide by $^{3}/_{8}$"-deep drawer track in the center of the drawer bottoms. Then, assemble the drawers with glue and nails. Make the end panels for the base cabinet and bookcase (see "Alternative Woodworking Techniques" pages 9-10). The only difference on these end panels is that there is no insert panel. Assemble the base cabinet top (see "Alternative Woodworking Techniques" page 11). Rout a $^{3}/_{8}$" roundover on the top and bottom front and left side edges of the base cabinet top. Put edge-banding on the door's and drawer front's edges.

13 | When you install the base cabinet, use shims to plumb and level the cabinet before you screw the cabinet to the wall with 2½" wood screws.

14 | When designing built-in cabinets, build the inside cabinet body ½" smaller than the face frame to allow for any walls that aren't perfectly square, so the face frame will still fit tightly against the wall as shown.

15 | With the base cabinet set in place, set the base top on the base cabinet. Use a pencil to scribe the base top to the wall. Trim the top as necessary.

16 | Screw the top to the base cabinet with 1¼" screws.

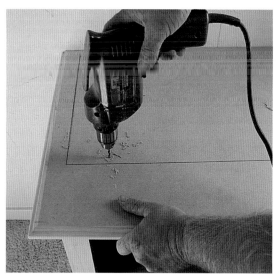

17 Temporarily place the bookcase onto the base cabinet and trace a line around the bookcase onto the base cabinet top. Remove the bookcase and predrill screw holes for attaching the bookcase to the base cabinet.

18 Screw the bookcase to the base cabinet with 1½" screws.

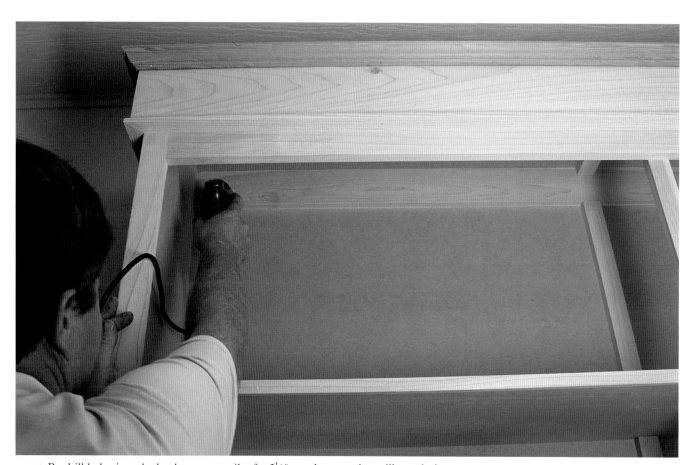

19 Predrill holes into the bookcase top nailer for 2½" wood screws that will attach the bookcase to the interior wall framing studs. Countersink the screw holes. This allows you to fill the screw holes after you have inserted the screws through the nailer and into the studs.

20 | Install the crown moulding on the base cabinet under the front edges of the base top and install the quarter-round at the base of the bookcase and the base cabinet top. Attach the base moulding with nails. Cut and nail on wall trim to cover the gaps between the cabinet and the wall.

21 | To achieve a truly custom built-in look, use paintable latex caulking and caulk all gaps and seams as necessary. This is probably one of the most important steps for a paint-finished cabinet as it creates a seamless fit between the wall and the cabinet. After the cabinet, doors and drawerfronts have been painted, hang the doors and attach the drawer fronts to the front of the drawer boxes. Attach the pulls and you're ready to fill the cabinet and bookshelves with all your treasures.

project kids toy plans

I've included two sets of plans for some of the toys that the kids like to make. The toys are pre-cut to rough shape. Then cutting lines are drawn on the blanks for the kids to follow and finish cutting out the toys. They then drill, sand, glue and screw the projects together.

PADDLE BOAT

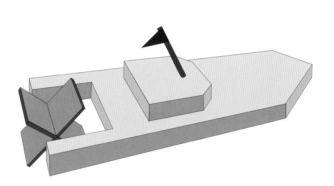

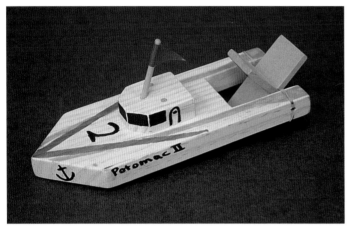

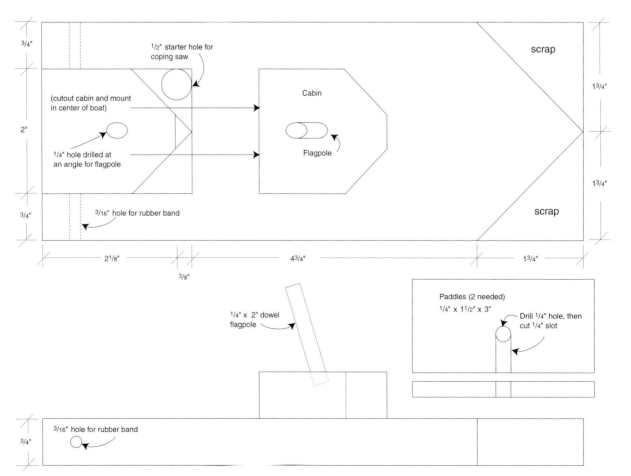

3/4"

1/2" starter hole for
coping saw

scrap

(cutout cabin and mount
in center of boat)

1 3/4"

Cabin

2"

1/4" hole drilled at
an angle for flagpole

Flagpole

3/4"

3/16" hole for rubber band

1 3/4"

scrap

2 1/8"

4 3/4"

1 3/4"

3/8"

1/4" x 2" dowel
flagpole

Paddles (2 needed)
1/4" x 1 1/2" x 3"

Drill 1/4" hole, then
cut 1/4" slot

3/16" hole for rubber band

3/4"

FORMULA ONE RACECAR

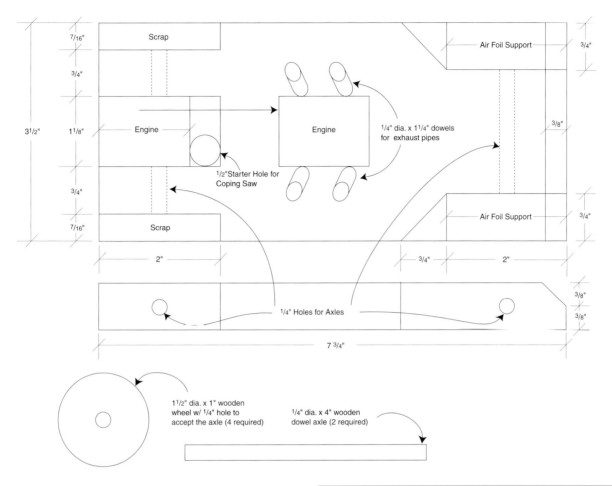

Scrap

Air Foil Support 3/4"

7/16"

3/4"

3 1/2"   1 1/8"   Engine

Engine

1/4" dia. x 1 1/4" dowels for exhaust pipes

3/8"

1/2"Starter Hole for Coping Saw

3/4"

7/16"   Scrap

Air Foil Support   3/4"

2"   3/4"   2"

3/8"
3/8"

1/4" Holes for Axles

7 3/4"

1 1/2" dia. x 1" wooden wheel w/ 1/4" hole to accept the axle (4 required)

1/4" dia. x 4" wooden dowel axle (2 required)

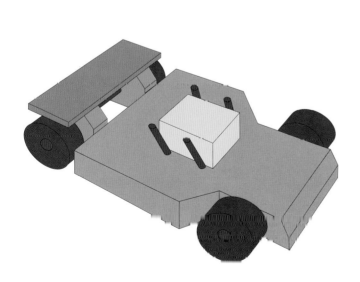

index